ACCESS DENIED

ACCESS DENIED

How Internet Filters Impact Student Learning in High Schools

Lynn Sutton

CAMBRIA
PRESS

YOUNGSTOWN, NEW YORK

No part of this publication may be reproduced, stored in or introduced into a retrieval system, or transmitted, in any form, or by any means (electronic, mechanical, photo-copying, recording, or otherwise), without the prior permission of the publisher. Requests for permission should be directed to permissions@cambriapress.com, or mailed to Permissions, Cambria Press, PO Box 350, Youngstown, New York 14174-0350.
ISBN-10: 1-934043-07-9
ISBN-13: 978-1-934043-07-3

Library of Congress Cataloging-in-Publication Data

Sutton, Lynn Sorensen.
    Access denied : how Internet filters impact student learning in high
    schools / Lynn Sutton.
       p. cm.
    Includes bibliographical references and index.
    ISBN-13: 978-1-934043-07-3 (alk. paper)
    1. Internet in education--United States. 2. Internet—Access control
    —United States. 3. Internet and teenagers—United States.
    4. Freedom of information—United States.   I. Title.
    LB1044.87.S88 2006
    373.133'44678—dc22

                                                        2006032903

To my family

TABLE OF CONTENTS

LIST OF FIGURES

FOREWORD

Every new medium for human expression inspires both excitement and anxiety. No sooner was the Internet upon us in the 1990s than anxiety arose over the ease of accessing pornography and other controversial content. In response, entrepreneurs soon developed filtering products. By the end of the decade, a new industry had emerged to create and market Internet filters.

The filters were highly imprecise. The problem was intrinsic to the technology. The sheer size of the Internet meant that identifying potentially offensive content had to be done mechanically, by matching "key" words and phrases; hence, the blocking of websites for "Middle sex County," "Beaver College," and "*breast* cancer"—just three of the better-known among thousands of early examples of overly broad, and indeed irrational, filtering.

Some people argued that inaccuracy was an acceptable cost of keeping the Internet safe, especially for kids. Others—including many librarians, educators, and civil libertarians—argued that the cost was too high. To help inform this policy debate, the Free Expression Policy Project

(FEPP) published *Internet Filters: A Public Policy Report* in the fall of 2001, summarizing the results of more than 70 empirical studies on the performance of filters. These studies ranged from anecdotal accounts of blocked sites to extensive research applying social science methods.

Nearly every study revealed substantial overblocking. That is, even taking into account that filter manufacturers use broad and vague blocking categories—for example, "violence," "tasteless / gross," or "lifestyle"—their products arbitrarily blocked many web pages that had no relation to the disapproved content categories.

Despite such irrational results, the filtering business continued to grow. Schools and offices installed filters on their computers, and public libraries came under pressure to do so. In December 2000, President Bill Clinton signed the "Children's Internet Protection Act" (or "CIPA"), which despite its child-focused title, mandated filters on *all* computers—whether used by minors or adults—in schools and libraries that receive federal aid for online connections.

Although the Supreme Court upheld CIPA in 2003, the debate over Internet filters is far from over. For one thing, the Court only turned back a constitutional challenge to the law as written. It left open the possibility of lawsuits challenging CIPA "as applied" by particular schools or libraries.

For another thing, schools and libraries, at least in theory, have the option of offering unfiltered Internet access by refusing federal aid. They need information about how filters operate in order to make this decision.

Finally, parents, employers, universities, and others not covered by CIPA also need solid information in order to make wise choices about censorship and free expression online—and especially about the perils of filtering technology.

Because the issue remains important, FEPP published a fully revised and updated edition of *Internet Filters* in 2006. It was during our research for this revised report that we discovered Dr. Lynn Sutton's study of the effects of filtering in one typical American school. Dr. Sutton's report was particularly useful because it was qualitative, not quantitative. That is, it did not reduce the adverse effects of filters to percentages and statistics, as many other tests and studies attempted to do—in the process, often understating if not ignoring the actual content and value of the tens of thousands of websites that filters routinely block, even at their narrowest settings. Dr. Sutton's work gives immediacy to the filtering story, and shows through real-world experiences how damaging filters can be for the educational process. It is cause for celebration that her work is now appearing in book form.

Internet filtering today suffers from two major flaws. Stated bluntly, they are: bias and absurdity. Bias arises because like all of us, filter manufacturers have their own ideas about what kind of expression is valuable, acceptable, or inoffensive, and what kind of expression, by contrast, is offensive, unacceptable, or "harmful to minors." In a free society, everybody is entitled to have a personal view on these matters, but government cannot enforce one view by silencing all others. When censorship decisions are made by private companies, however, the First Amendment does not ordinarily apply. Filters thus have the potential to suppress speech much more broadly than any law or government policy could do.

Private biases are evident both in the blocking categories that filtering companies establish and the specific blocking decisions that company employees make. Some filters block virtually all information about gay and lesbian issues, regardless of whether it has sexual content. Some have broad blocking categories for "alternative lifestyles," "cults," or "sex education"; what qualifies as an acceptable mainstream religion, and what merits "cult" status, of course, involves highly subjective judgments. Not surprisingly, one of the most frequently and deliberately blocked categories has been criticism of filtering software.

The absurdity of filtering results is an even more insidious problem. Reducing human expression to simplistic categories and sets of key words and phrases is bound to lead to large volumes of "false positives"—blocks that result from the inability of even the most sophisticated "artificial intelligence" algorithms to consider the context, meaning, and value of speech. The examples are legion, from the early blocking by CYBER-sitter of the word "homosexual" in the sentence "The Catholic Church opposes homosexual marriage"—thus leaving the viewer to read that "The Catholic Church opposes marriage" —to the blocking of Congress-man *Dick* Armey's website, the University of Kansas's Archie R. *Dykes* Medical Library, and the phrase "at least 21" from a human rights site reporting that at least 21 people were killed or wounded in an incident in Indonesia ("at least 21" being a phrase that is often blocked because it is likely to appear on pornography sites).[1]

Some of the most dramatic evidence of absurd overblocking came to light in the course of the lawsuit brought by the American Library Associa-tion and other groups to challenge CIPA. A three-judge federal court that heard the evidence explained that initially, filters trawl the web much as search engines do, "harvesting" for possibly relevant sites by looking for key words and phrases. There follows a process of "winnowing," which also relies largely on mechanical techniques. Although most filter compa-nies also use some human review, their relatively small staffs (between eight and a few dozen people) can give at most a cursory review to a fraction of the sites that are harvested each day.

The three-judge court found that as a result of their operation, filters mistakenly block tens of thousands of valuable web pages. Focusing on the filters used most often in libraries, the judges gave dozens of exam-ples, among them a Knights of Columbus site, misidentified by Cyber Patrol as "adult / sexually explicit"; a site on fly fishing, misidentified by Bess as "pornography"; a guide to allergies and a site opposing the death penalty, both blocked by Bess as "pornography"; a site for aspiring dentists, blocked by Cyber Patrol as "adult/sexually explicit"; and a site that sells religious wall hangings, blocked by WebSense as "sex."

---

[1] Citations for all facts and quotations in this Foreword can be found in *Internet Filters: A Public Policy Report*, www.fepproject.org/policyreports/filters2.pdf.

The judges noted also that filters frequently block all pages on a site, no matter how innocent, based on a "root url." The root urls for large sites like Yahoo or Geocities contain not only reams of educational material, but thousands of personal web pages. Likewise, according to the court, one item of disapproved content (for example, a sexuality column on Salon.com) often results in filtering the entire site.

In large part because of this massive overblocking—because of the sheer absurdity of the results produced by filters—the three-judge court struck down CIPA's library provisions. (No suit was brought to challenge the law as applied to schools.) The judges found that there are less burdensome ways for libraries to address concerns about illegal obscenity on the Internet, and about minors' access to material that most adults consider inappropriate for them, including "acceptable use" policies and supervision by library staff.

In reversing this lower court decision and upholding the constitutionality of CIPA in 2003, Chief Justice William Rehnquist (writing for a "plurality" of four of the nine Supreme Court justices) asserted that library patrons have no right to unfiltered Internet access. That is, according to Rehnquist, filtering is no different in principle from librarians' decisions not to select certain books for library shelves. Moreover, Rehnquist said, because the government is providing financial aid for Internet access, it can limit the scope of the information that is made available. He added that if erroneous blocking of "completely innocuous" sites creates a First Amendment problem, "any such concerns are dispelled" by a provision in CIPA that allows libraries to disable their filters upon request, for "bona fide research or other lawful purposes."

Supreme Court Justices Anthony Kennedy and Stephen Breyer wrote separate opinions concurring in the judgment upholding CIPA. Both relied on the "disabling" provisions of the law as a way for libraries to avoid restricting adults' access to the Internet. Kennedy emphasized that if librarians fail to unblock on request, or adults are otherwise burdened in their searches, then a lawsuit challenging CIPA "as applied" to that situation might be appropriate.

Three justices—John Paul Stevens, David Souter, and Ruth Bader Ginsburg—dissented from the Supreme Court decision. Their dissents drew attention to the three-judge court's description of the perils of filtering, and to the delays and other burdens that make discretionary disabling a poor substitute for uncensored Internet access. Souter objected to Rehnquist's analogy between filters and library book selection, arguing that filtering is actually more akin to "buying an encyclopedia and then cutting out pages." Stevens noted that censorship is not necessarily constitutional just because it is a condition of government funding—especially when funded programs are supposed to facilitate free expression, as in universities and libraries.

After the Supreme Court upheld CIPA, public libraries confronted a stark choice—forgo federal aid for Internet connections, including e-rate discounts, or invest resources in a filtering system that censors large quantities of valuable material. Public schools, not having challenged CIPA, confronted this dilemma from the moment the law was enacted. But because of local political pressures, most school districts had already bought into filtering. As one school official frankly noted: "It would be politically disastrous for us not to filter. All the good network infrastructure we've installed would come down with the first instance of an elementary school student accessing some of the absolutely raunchy sites out there."

This administrator's observation points up the high political stakes in the filtering debate. On the one hand, filters are highly effective, if often irrational, censorship tools, blatantly aimed at suppressing information and ideas. On the other hand, political leaders and the general public continue to express fears about minors' access to pornography or other presumably inappropriate speech online.

There is no simple answer to this political dilemma, which has produced a financial windfall for filtering company executives. Speech can be powerful, and the human impulse to censor words, images, and ideas that are thought to be wrong and dangerous is understandable. There are, of course, the classic free-society responses—education of our youth to be critical thinkers; "more speech" in the marketplace of ideas where good ideas supposedly drive out bad ones. But these solutions lack the emotional satisfactions and broad "quick-fix" appeal of censorship.

Among the more "realpolitik" arguments, some critics of filters emphasize that they create a false sense of security because smart youngsters can circumvent them, and because they "underblock" – that is, they fail to identify and suppress many "bad" sites. But these practical arguments cede too much ideological territory to the advocates of censorship, and lead the public to conclude that if only we can improve filtering technology, the solution to our worries will be at hand.

This is where reports "from the trenches" such as Lynn Sutton's come in. By describing the experiences of ordinary students and teachers, Sutton demonstrates the negative impact of filters on research, discovery, and curiosity—the essential elements of education. Stories like those that Sutton recounts have the potential to persuade local communities that simple training in Internet safety serves all of us better than a filtered Internet.

Meanwhile, as FEPP's report concluded, there are steps that schools and libraries subject to CIPA, as well as companies and parents that want to filter, can take to reduce both the bias and absurdity of filtering products.

First, they should understand the differences among products, and choose filters that easily permit both overall disabling and unblocking of individual sites.

Second, they should only activate the minimum necessary blocking categories, rather than accepting the filter's default setting. For schools and libraries, this means only activating the "pornography" or similar filtering category, since CIPA only requires blocking of obscenity, child pornography, and "harmful to minors" material. Each of these legal categories requires that the targeted material contain "prurient" or "lascivious" sexual content. Thus, neither sex education, nor political discussion of sexual issues, nor sexually explicit health sites, need to be blocked to comply with CIPA.

Third, schools and libraries subject to CIPA should promptly disable filters on request from adults or, if permitted by the portion of the law that applies to them, from minors as well.

Finally, all of us need to educate ourselves and each other about non-censorship approaches to online literacy and safety. Despite the superficial appeal of filters, they are not a solution to concerns about pornography or other questionable content online. Media literacy, sex education, and free speech are the best ways to protect the next generation.

Marjorie Heins

Fellow, Brennan Center for Justice

Founder & Coordinator, Free Expression Policy Project

This Foreword was adapted from Marjorie Heins's Introduction to *Internet Filters: A Public Policy Report* (Free Expression Policy Project, Brennan Center for Justice, 2006).

PREFACE

Since the original research was done for my doctoral dissertation in the spring of 2004, the topic of Internet filtering in libraries has gone to the back burner. After a flurry of post-mortem news stories following the surprising ruling of the U.S. Supreme Court that upheld the constitutionality of the Children's Internet Protection Act (CIPA), the attention of the intellectual freedom community in libraries went elsewhere. And yet, today more than ever libraries need guidance on how to live in a post-CIPA world. They need to learn how to minimize the limitations of filtering in order to provide as much of the world of information as possible to their users.

Most of the library literature that has appeared in the last two years has been geared to public libraries. CIPA has forced public libraries to make very difficult Sophie-type choices. They must either forego considerable amounts of federal funding in the form of e-rate discounts and grants (which ironically all too often provide the only means of buying computers for the public to use) or invest in filtering systems that they know will result in large amounts of legitimate, constitutionally-protected speech being denied to their patrons. More libraries than not have chosen to install filters. Comer (2005) surveyed the public libraries in Indiana and found that 18 per cent of the respondents had modified their computer usage policies because of CIPA. Regrettably, the city council of one major American city ("Phoenix council demands filters," 2004) went beyond CIPA in preventing adults from choosing to disable the filter, as required by law.

Jaeger, Bertot and McClure (2004) provide an excellent analysis of the issues facing public libraries in the post-CIPA environment. Such issues include filter disabling mechanisms, staffing costs, technology costs, digital divide complications and legal challenges on the application of CIPA in individual libraries. Minow (2004) offers practical guidance to libraries trying to live within CIPA as well as detailed insights on the likelihood of as-applied challenges to CIPA and the intricacies of the disabling provision obligation for libraries.

Due to technical reasons, school media centers were not included in the American Library Association's legal challenge to CIPA, so for them, there was no change when the U.S. Supreme Court upheld the law. The vast majority of school media centers filtered before the ruling and the vast majority of school media centers still do. However, School Library Journal ("Feds restart filter debate," 2006) points out the ironic twist in the news report that the Department of Justice, which fought so hard in CIPA to prove that filters were effective and not overly harmful, is now arguing that filters are not effective enough to keep children safe and therefore the more extreme measures of the Child Online Protection Act (COPA) are necessary. COPA has remained stalled in federal court since its passage.

It was never the intent of this project to systematically study the effectiveness of filtering devices. However, such information provides a valuable backdrop to qualitative studies such as mine that look at the effect of filtering on student learning. Heins, Cho and Feldman (2006) provide an excellent summary of the most recent empirical studies on filtering effectiveness, updating a previous (2001) report. They conclude that filters still overblock and underblock and their widespread use results in a serious threat to the fundamental values of free expression.

My original study was undertaken because there was a lack of research on the impact of Internet filters on student learning. That is still the case. Nearly everyone else focuses on the legal arguments or the technical effectiveness or the philosophical First Amendment debate. The limitations of my study are evident: it is one filter in one school district with one predominant socioeconomic class. However, the qualitative methods that were used dig deeply into what is actually going on in that school and reveal the severe frustrations of students and teachers alike. More research is certainly welcome that is broader in scope and sample size. But my prediction is that the results will be the same.

ACKNOWLEDGEMENTS

I am indebted to many people for their help and encouragement throughout this project. The staff and students of the high school where the original research was done must be commended for their cooperation and candor. I hope the publication of this work will enable school officials across the country to recognize themselves in Lakeside High School and re-examine their practices.

Karen Tonso has been an outstanding teacher, mentor, and friend from the first day I walked into her office. Linda Tillman, who joined me in North Carolina, gave me confidence to pursue my work and both challenged and encouraged me. Bob Holley has served variously as boss, colleague, friend and mentor and could always be counted on for frank advice. Susan Fino awakened in me a love for constitutional law and made me wish I had gone to law school right out of college.

Completing this research project was only accomplished through the love of a supportive family. To my mom, I hope I have earned the pride you show in me. To my children, Elizabeth, Alexander and Derek, with your patience and support, I could not fail. To my husband, Bill, I could not have attempted, much less completed, this research and subsequent book without your selfless love and support. I thank you all.

And finally, I am indebted to Toni Tan and the entire staff of Cambria Press for their patience, creativity and good humor. They made the entire book publishing experience a delight, even for a first-time author.

ACCESS DENIED

CHAPTER ONE

INTRODUCTION

STATEMENT OF THE PROBLEM

> Whenever I'm on the Internet here at school, there's always
> somebody walking around behind you, checking over your shoul-
> der to make sure you're not doing anything inappropriate. I think
> if you are going to learn, you have to do some inappropriate
> things. If you're learning history, you can't just learn what is
> proper, you have to go read what others have written and some
> of it may just be inappropriate. – High School Boy (Levin and
> Arafeh, 2002, p. 20)

This study involves the application of intellectual freedom in the school
setting. Intellectual freedom is the belief that human beings have the right
to receive information and express themselves freely. As such, intellectual
freedom is one of the most closely held core values of librarianship.

As a value, people of goodwill interpret intellectual freedom differently in terms of policy applications. These policy applications are often contested, debated and sometimes settled only in the courts, where defenders of the U.S. Constitution interpret and extend the First Amendment to situations and technologies wholly unknown to the founders who wrote the original documents.

The school library or media center "serves as a point of voluntary access to information and ideas and as a learning laboratory for students as they acquire critical thinking and problem solving skills needed in a pluralistic society" (Office for Intellectual Freedom [OIF], 2002, p. 105). School media centers provide support for the curriculum and also allow students to explore a wide range of topics of interest to them. Gardner (2001b) says that the school media center "is the *one* academic unit in each school district that serves every student regardless of their course selection or academic ability" (p. 23).

In recent years, one of the primary reasons that students use the school's media center is to access the Internet. The Internet has become a standard source of information and entertainment for today's youth. A recent study from the Pew Internet and American Life Project (Levin and Arafeh, 2002) found that 78% of America's children between the ages of 12 and 17 use the Internet and nearly every online teenager (94%) has used the Internet for school research.

In order to qualify for substantial federal e-rate discounts and other federal funds under the provisions of the Children's Internet Protection Act (CIPA), many schools use filtering technology on library computers. Studies indicate the numbers of schools using filtering technology range from 53% (Curry and Haycock, 2001) to over 90% (National School Boards Foundation, 2002). Filters block access to Internet content that has been pre-determined to be objectionable or inappropriate. The vast majority of content is intended to be blocked because it is sexually explicit, though chat rooms, e-mail and software downloads are also commonly blocked.

Because of the legal controversies surrounding CIPA in recent years, the literature has been filled with various kinds of studies and opinion pieces on the effectiveness of filters. The 2003 study conducted by the Electronic Frontier Foundation and the Online Policy Group is critical of the effectiveness of filters in educational institutions. The Kaiser study (Richardson, Resnick, Hansen, Derry and Rideout, 2002) demonstrates the difference that filter settings make in the amount of harmless material that is blocked through the use of filters. The Pew Internet and American Life Project study (Levin and Arafeh, 2002) demonstrates how technologically savvy students are becoming increasingly frustrated with the limitations of filtered Internet access and use in schools. One finding says that "while many students recognize the need and a desire to shelter teenagers from inappropriate material and adult-oriented commercial ads, they complain that blocking and filtering software raise significant barriers to their legitimate educational use of the Internet" (p. 19).

The use of filtering technology in libraries has been discouraged by the American Library Association (ALA) on First Amendment grounds, even though ALA was unsuccessful in its suit against the Children's Internet Protection Act. CIPA requires public libraries to install filters on all library computers in order to obtain commercial e-rate discounts for Internet access and certain categories of grants from the Library Services and Technology Act (LSTA). On June 23, 2003, the U.S. Supreme Court surprised many free speech activists by ruling CIPA constitutional (*U.S. v. American Library Association,* 2003), largely on the grounds that the filters could be disabled upon request. Therefore, school media centers, along with public libraries, remain subject to the filtering provisions of CIPA if they choose to accept e-rate discounts or LSTA funds.

Quantitative studies such as the Kaiser study (Richardson, et al., 2002) and Electronic Frontier Foundation and Online Policy Group (2003) have strengthened the knowledge base on how filters work and how effective they are in accomplishing owner objectives to block Internet content. What has still not been explored is the effect of filtering on the students' work and the experiences of students as they use filtered Internet computers. Policy makers in America's schools could benefit from research using ethnographic qualitative methods about the experiences of students using filtered Internet computers, which this study attempts to demonstrate.

PURPOSE OF THE STUDY

We know that the vast majority of American youth use the Internet for their schoolwork, such as term paper research. Most schools employ filtering technology on computers in media centers to block access to "objectionable" content. These filters are more or less successful, depending on how they have been configured. The use of filters raises the possibility that students' First Amendment rights are at risk by blocking access to constitutionally protected speech. What we still do not know is how students are actually affected when Internet filters are used to conduct term paper research. The purpose of this qualitative research is to study the experiences of high school students conducting term paper research with filtered Internet access in a suburban high school media center.

CHAPTER TWO

FRAMING THE QUESTION: A REVIEW OF THE RELEVANT LITERATURE

The focus of this research is the application of intellectual freedom in the school setting. Specifically, I will examine and describe the experiences of students who conduct term paper research with filtered Internet access in a suburban high school media center. To provide a framework for such a study, literature in three different areas of inquiry must be examined: Internet use in schools, filtering technology, and intellectual freedom in libraries.

Further, it is important to recognize that the nature of the literature in these three areas often takes more of a prescriptive and experiential, rather than research-based approach. Two researchers doing work in the area of Internet use in school libraries (Flowers, 1998; Gardner, 2001a) have both observed that the number of research studies in the field is small, compared with informational and opinion pieces. Gardner further notes that much of the extant literature, policy-making, and legislation, are aimed at public libraries. Some of these concepts apply to other types of libraries, notably publicly funded schools and universities, but some of the direct impact is lost.

INTERNET USE IN SCHOOLS

Tapscott (1998) has proclaimed, "The Net Generation has arrived" (p. 1). The current generation of primary and secondary students has grown up surrounded by digital media. They use it for information, education, entertainment, shopping, and virtually every other aspect of their lives. In the area of education, the Internet has come to be a standard and accepted tool in schools. According to the National Center for Education Statistics (Cattagni and Farris, 2001), 98% of public schools in the United States have access to the Internet. Significantly, the survey found virtually no differences in access by school characteristics such as poverty level or metropolitan status in 1999 or 2000. An unpublished study cited in the Pew Internet and American Life Project (Levin and Arafeh, 2002) found that 78% of America's children between the ages of 12 and 17 use the Internet, and nearly every online teenager (94%) has used the Internet for school research. Similar data were reported in a 2001 survey by the National Center for Education Statistics (DeBell and Chapman, 2003) where more than 90% of high school aged youth use computers, and at least 75% use the Internet.

School Media Centers

Almost all children in America attend a school that has a media center. According to the latest study from the National Center for Education Statistics (Holton, Bae, Baldridge, Brown, and Heffron, 2004), 97% of children in public schools and 82% of children in private schools attended a school with a library media center. School media centers play a strong role in the education of America's children. Gardner (2001b) lists four main missions of school libraries: to promote literature and reading; to provide information that supports the curriculum; to teach young people how to find, process and use information; and to provide information students will need as they grow into adulthood. Shirley (2001) posits that it was the threat of Sputnik in 1957 and the publication of *A Nation at Risk* (National Commission on Excellence in Education, 1983) that prompted the development of full-service school libraries designed to serve the diverse learning needs of students.

School media centers have changed radically in recent years, moving from a focus on resources to an emphasis on lifelong learning. The landmark publication *Information Power: Guidelines for School Library Media Programs* (American Association of School Librarians and Association for Educational Communications and Technology [AASL and AECT], 1988) brought the concept of information literacy to the forefront as a way to encourage lifelong learning in students. The information literate student understands the need for information as well as how to identify, access, and use it in all aspects of his / her life. Later works, such as *Information Power: Building Partnerships for Learning* (AASL and AECT, 1998) emphasize the collaboration that must take place among all partners in learning: administrators, teachers, librarians, parents and other community members, for a culture of lifelong learning to flourish.

Library media specialists play a number of integral roles in this process of nurturing lifelong learners (AASL and AECT, 1998). As teachers, they instruct students on ways to analyze and meet their information needs. As instructional partners, they collaborate with others to work across the curriculum with a wide variety of resources. As information specialists, they are experts in acquiring and evaluating information in new technologies. And finally, as program administrators, media specialists define or influence policies and direct the library media program to achieve the larger educational goals of the school.

Library Research Service first studied the impact of school librarians on academic achievement in Colorado (Lance, 1994) and then replicated that study in a number of other states, most recently Michigan (Rodney, Lance and Hamilton-Pennell, 2003). They claim, "Decades of library media research findings indicate that one major factor that has demonstrated consistently a positive, strong, and statistically significant relationship to quality teaching is a close working relationship between the classroom teacher and the library media specialist" (p. 15). In particular, the Michigan study found that "the state's high school librarians have a measurable, positive, and statistically significant impact on MEAP test scores that cannot be explained away by other conditions for which data are available" (p. 78). Using multiple regression analysis, they determined, "alone, school librarian hours per 100 students explains 2.7% of the variation in test scores" (p.88). This may be compared to the percentage of students eligible for the National School Lunch Program, which explains 39% of the variation, percentage of minority students explaining 5.1%, and per pupil school expenditures, explaining 3.1%.

In recent years, one of the primary reasons that students use the school's media center is to access the Internet. Farmer (2002) describes observing high school students standing in line for twenty minutes to use an electronic encyclopedia, rather than resorting to the print version located near the computer. Lorenzen (2001) describes the confusion that high school students experience when left on their own to navigate the Web for research purposes. Librarians in schools have made progress in teaching students to use the Internet effectively as a powerful information tool. Craver (1998) describes successful instructional strategies for teaching Internet skills to high school students in order to prepare them for future research at the college level. Grant (2002) has posted Internet lessons online to share with peers, complete with PowerPoint slides, teaching instructions, handouts and evaluation checklist.

Librarians are also constantly vigilant of their responsibilities for ethical leadership in the Internet age. Johnson (2004) names five major ethical challenges for school library media specialists, filtering being first among them. The future of academic information is in the electronic format, thus it behooves media specialists and all other educators to teach secondary students the skills needed to access and use the power of electronic information. Research questions in this study will examine how students use the Internet for term paper research in a high school media center.

The Digital Divide

The term "digital divide" came into use during the Clinton administration. Clinton's National Telecommunications and Information Administration (NTIA) published a four-part series, *Falling through the Net* (1995, 1998, 1999, 2000) that defined the digital divide as the difference in access to digital information that separates the information-rich from the information-poor. Those without ready access to digital resources were predictably minorities, the less educated, and lower-income individuals. The purpose of the report was to understand the phenomenon of "haves" and "have-nots" as the first step in bridging the difference.

A recent report from the Pew Internet and American Life Project (Lenhart et al., 2003) confirms and updates the digital divide categories of the NTIA reports of the late 1990's. Growth in new Internet users has finally slowed, with a penetration rate hovering between 57% and 61%. Again, the groups that fall into the digital divide are those who are not white, not rich, and not highly educated. Interestingly, the gender gap seems to be finally bridged, as Internet use in America is exactly 50% male and 50% female.

A third report from the National Center for Education Statistics (DeBell and Chapman, 2003) confirms the categories of the digital divide: minorities, lower income families, and the less educated. It goes on to demonstrate how schools are one of the social institutions that have begun to bridge the digital divide.

> Among the group of children and adolescents who access the Internet at only one location, 52% of those from families in poverty and 59% of those whose parents have not earned at least a high school credential do so at school. In comparison, 26% of those from families not in

> poverty and 39% of those with more highly educated parents do so only at school. This illustrates the role of schools in bridging the digital divide. (p. vi)

The earlier NTIA reports (1995, 1998, 1999, 2000) indicate the role that libraries play in bridging the digital divide is of primary importance. The public library may be the only access that the poorest of the poor have to information that is published electronically. Implications of the digital divide come into play in this study of Internet filters in high school media centers. Poor, non-white children are much more likely to rely on libraries, especially school libraries, for Internet access. When that access is filtered to a less than comprehensive version of the Internet, the question becomes, what is being left out? Filtering companies offer blocking for many categories of subject material other than the illegal categories of obscenity, child pornography, and "materials harmful to minors." Moral and political viewpoints are often commonly blocked such as information on homosexuality, sex education in general, gun control, smoking, hate speech, abortion, and contraception. Thus, poor children who have no other recourse than library computers are blocked from accessing information that they need and have every legal right to obtain, because someone thought they were "safer" without it. In my study, one research question will consider to what extent students are affected by the limitations imposed by a mandatory filtering system that provides less than comprehensive access to Internet resources.

FILTERING TECHNOLOGY

How Filters Work

For the purposes of this study, filtering technology is defined as commercial computer software that limits, blocks, or restricts access to Internet content. Filters block access to Internet content that has been pre-determined to be objectionable or inappropriate. The vast majority of content is blocked because it is sexually explicit, though chat rooms, e-mail and software downloads are also formats that are commonly blocked. Ayre (2004) provides a comprehensive study of the current status of filtering technology. Filters use several methods for blocking data: word blocking, which matches Web pages against a list of keywords, and site blocking, which matches URLs against a list of predetermined sites (Rosenberg, 2001). Web sites are put into categories by filtering companies and it is these categories that may be adjusted by the local filter administrator. However, most filtering companies are reluctant to list specific Web sites by category, claiming that is proprietary information. This makes it difficult to move a specific site from a misplaced category to a more suitable category. To some extent, what is blocked is a reflection of the intended market for the filtering product.

The U.S. Congress has appointed two separate commissions to study the use of filtering technology to protect children from materials inappropriate to minors. On October 20, 2000, the Commission on Online Child Protection presented its final report (COPA, 2000) to Congress. The report stated that the best Internet filtering technologies can be highly effective in directly blocking access to content that is harmful to minors, but noted that there are significant concerns about First Amendment issues when filters are used in libraries and schools. The second commission to study the use of Internet filtering technology was the "Committee to Study Tools and Strategies for Protecting Kids from Pornography and Their Applicability to Other Inappropriate Internet Content" of the Computer Science and Telecommunications Board of the National Research Council. This landmark study (Thornburgh, 2002) considers all sides of this complex issue. One of the study's findings is that, due to the nature of filters, "underblocking" and "overblocking"[2] errors are inevitable. The Committee states, "While the issue of underblocking and

---

[2] Overblocking occurs when an appropriate site is mistakenly deemed inappropriate and blocked from the user. Underblocking occurs when an inappropriate site is mistakenly deemed appropriate and is permitted to the user.

overblocking should not, in and of itself, rule out filters as a useful tool, the extent of underblocking and overblocking is a significant factor in understanding and deciding about the use of filters" (p. 277). They go on to note that legal challenges to government-mandated filters focus primarily on underblocking and overblocking problems. In the end, one of their conclusions is that social and educational strategies, rather than technological strategies such as filters, are most useful.

In addition, Congress also requested the National Telecommunications and Information Agency (NTIA) to "(1) evaluate whether the technology measures currently available adequately address the needs of educational institutions, and (2) evaluate the development and effectiveness of local Internet safety policies" (NTIA, 2003, p. 5). After balancing the importance of allowing children to use the Internet with the importance of protecting children from inappropriate material, the report concludes that currently available technology measures (filters) have the capacity to meet most, if not all, needs and concerns of educational institutions, although educators have significant concerns with underblocking and overblocking.

Meanwhile, schools have increasingly installed filtering technology for the protection of their students. Since 2001, the Children's Internet Protection Act (CIPA) requires schools receiving the Federal Communication Commission's Universal Service e-rate discount to install "technology protection measures" (i.e., filters) on computers with Internet access. According to Cattagni and Farris (2001), the e-rate program has been largely responsible for the increase in Internet access in public schools over the years. Even before 2001, many schools debated the pros and cons of Internet filters. As early as 1996, in a debate sponsored by the online journal *Electronic School,* Trotter (1996) anticipated schools across the nation opening up Internet access to their students, only to limit its use out of inappropriate fear of preoccupation with pornography, hate groups, and violence. On the other side, Splitt (1996) foresaw the constitutional problems that would inevitably arise from any official act by the government to limit free speech. Jost (2001) and Pownell and Bailey (1999) present even-handed analyses of the advantages and disadvantages of filters in school libraries. They reason that the reduced chances of a student accessing "inappropriate" material must be balanced against the knowledge that any kind of commercial filter will almost certainly block appropriate material, with a corresponding risk of violating the student's First Amendment rights. On the other end of the political spectrum, free speech advocates (Callister and Burbules, 2003; Kranich, 2004; Willard, 2003) are very open in labeling filters as over-protective and damaging in the long run.

There are indications that technologically savvy students are becoming increasingly frustrated with limitations on their Internet access in schools. Levin and Arafeh (2002) used qualitative methods to describe the attitudes and behaviors of students using the Internet in public schools. One finding from their study says that "while many students recognize the need and a desire to shelter teenagers from inappropriate material and adult-oriented commercial ads, they complain that blocking and filtering software raise significant barriers to their legitimate educational use of the Internet" (p. 19). A research question in the study will examine what sorts of barriers students encounter using filtered computers and how they try to overcome them.

Because of the legal controversies surrounding the Children's Internet Protection Act in recent years, the literature has been filled with various kinds of studies and opinion pieces on the effectiveness of filters. The Kaiser study (Richardson, et al., 2002) demonstrates the difference that filter settings make in the amount of harmless material that is blocked through the use of filters. The study was particularly notable for having been published in *JAMA* (Journal of the American Medical Association). Given their medical backgrounds, the authors focused on adolescents' use of the Internet for health concerns. The objective of the study was to measure how much pornography-blocking software used in schools and libraries limits access to health information Web sites. They write:

> The use of filtering software in public schools and libraries
> is of special concern, because adolescents' health concerns
> often focus on issues related to sexuality, and because those
> who do not have computers at home rely on schools and
> libraries for Internet access. (p. 2888)

They noted the surprising lack of empirical studies on blocking errors. They simulated searching of health information questions, as well as pornographic searches, using six filters commonly used in schools and libraries. The results showed only minimal overblocking of legitimate health sites at the "least restrictive" level, but significantly more over-blocking at the "most restrictive" level. The amount of overblocking varied according to topic. "Safe sex" was blocked much more exten-sively than other topics, such as breast cancer. The authors warn,

> There may be principled reasons why some schools or
> libraries choose to block more than pornography, includ-
> ing some kinds of health information. These decisions,
> however, should be viewed as important policy decisions
> and not mere technical configuration issues to be left to
> network administrators. (p. 2893)

One research question in the study will explore to what extent outside influences from teachers or school administrators (other people's parents) have on day-to-day library research needs by students.

The way in which the Kaiser study has been interpreted in the field reveals the dichotomy of opinion on the subject of filters. In a statement on the Kaiser study, noted free speech activist Nancy Willard (2002) emphasized the dangers of overblocking at the most restrictive level and states "this study clearly demonstrates the concerns about placing reliance on filtering software" (p. 3). On the other hand, H. Auld, author of the article "Filters work: Get over it" in *American Libraries*

(2003) believed that the study's findings indicated that filters, when operated at their least restrictive setting, posed only a minor impediment to searching for health information. Thus, the level of filter settings can be identified as a key element in the overall effectiveness of a filtering program. Haycock (2001) reports,

> The level of satisfaction with the software and vendor was very much dependent on whether the program tended to block too much or too little, whether the filtering was done on-site or off-site, and whether the teacher-librarian had any control and ability to override the system. (p. 241)

The 2003 study conducted by the Electronic Frontier Foundation and the Online Policy Group is critical of the effectiveness of filters in educational institutions, as might be expected from unabashed civil rights organizations. They carried out their study because "no organization has studied effectively and quantitatively the issue of student Internet access within public schools that operate Internet blocking software" (p. 3). Their methodology involved selecting topics from the mandated curricula of three states, generating search strings from the topics, recording up to 50 Web pages that resulted from these search strings, and then testing the Web pages against Internet blocking software (filters). After testing nearly one million Web pages, one of their key findings states:

> Schools that implement Internet blocking software even with the least restrictive settings will block at a minimum tens of thousands of Web pages inappropriately, either because the Web pages are miscategorized or because the Web pages, while correctly categorized, do not merit blocking. (p. 25)

The study portrays the effect of filtering on students in this way: "biases and mistakes inherent in Internet blocking software reduce the student's access to materials directly related to state-mandated curriculum topics in school without adequately shielding the students from objectionable content" (p. 74). Significantly for my research, the authors note that their study "serves as groundwork for a potential in-depth future study within the schools that will investigate how students use the Internet within the educational environment and how blocking software affects this use" (p. 75).

First Amendment Issues

Any complete discussion of the literature on filtering technology must include an accounting of legal challenges to government-ordered restrictions on Internet speech. Kaiser (2000) provides an early analysis of the constitutional issues involved in the use of Internet filters as applied to public schools. While minors have lesser First Amendment rights than adults, nevertheless, their rights remain substantial. Congress' first attempt to protect minors from indecent online speech was the Communications Decency Act of 1996, which was ultimately struck down by the Supreme Court as a violation of the First Amendment. Congress next tried to tailor more narrowly the language of the Child Online Protection Act (COPA) to withstand a constitutional challenge. However, COPA has never been implemented. The Supreme Court has twice upheld injunctions by the Circuit Court without ruling directly on its constitutionality (*Ashcroft v. American Civil Liberties Union*, 2004). It is now back in Circuit Court, where the government must show under the strict scrutiny test that the law employs the least restrictive means of achieving a compelling government interest.

Nancy Willard (2002) provides an accounting of the failures of the Children's Internet Protection Act, as Congress' third attempt to protect children from obscenity, child pornography, and material harmful to minors. Again, the legislation was struck down in District Court, with a ruling that the federal requirement for filtering software violates the constitutional rights of library patrons, both children and adults. As noted above, the legal challenge by the American Library Association and

American Civil Liberties Union specifically did *not* include public schools. Because school libraries do not receive federal funds directly, but rather through their individual schools, and because these schools are not themselves members of the American Library Association, neither the ALA nor school libraries had legal standing to bring suit on this issue. Since CIPA was ruled constitutional in June, 2003 by the U.S. Supreme Court as it applied to public libraries, the chance of a successful legal challenge on the part of schools is remote. Therefore, school media centers also remain subject to the filtering provisions of CIPA if they accept e-rate or certain categories of LSTA funds.

INTELLECTUAL FREEDOM IN LIBRARIES

Intellectual freedom comes into play when the free speech principles of the First Amendment are applied in the practical setting of libraries. Intellectual freedom, the belief that human beings have the right to receive information and express themselves freely, is a core value of librarianship. Professional librarians, embodied by the American Library Association, are fierce defenders of intellectual freedom. The foundation piece for any serious study of intellectual freedom issues in libraries is ALA's *Intellectual Freedom Manual* (Office for Intellectual Freedom, 2002). The *Manual* is a systematic compilation of history, policies, interpretations, and current issues updates on the topic of intellectual freedom. The core of the work is the "Library Bill of Rights" and its official interpretations, which are the major policy statements for the entire profession. One such interpretation of the Library Bill of Rights, the "Universal Right to Free Expression," reveals the strength of librarians' commitment to intellectual freedom:

> The American Library Association is unswerving in its commitment to human rights and intellectual freedom; the two are inseparably linked and inextricably entwined. Freedom of opinion and expression is not derived from

or dependent on any form of government or political
power. This right is inherent in every individual. It cannot be surrendered, nor can it be denied. True justice comes
from the exercise of this right. (p. 194)

While early challenges to free speech in libraries typically involved
removing individual books from the shelf, use of the Internet in libraries
has raised entirely new questions. The best introduction to modern
technology-based legal challenges to intellectual freedom in libraries is
Robert Peck's *Libraries, the First Amendment and Cyberspace: What
You Need to Know* (2000). He clearly distinguishes the legal definitions
of "obscenity" and "pornography," delineates the rights of children sepa-
rately from adults, and clarifies the doctrine of a public forum, which is a
critical concept in the legal history of intellectual freedom in libraries. He
provides a context for the most important court cases in the field: *Miller
v. California* (1973) set the criteria currently in effect for the definition
of obscenity. In *Board of Education, Island Trees Union Free School
District No. 26 v. Pico* (1982), the Supreme Court ruled that school
boards may not remove books from school library shelves for political or
partisan purposes. The Communications Decency Act was declared
unconstitutional by the Supreme Court in *Reno v. American Civil Liberties
Union* (1997). In *Kathleen R v. City of Livermore* (1999), a mother sued
unsuccessfully to force her public library to filter its computers so her
son could not access pornography. In *Mainstream Loudon v. Board of
Trustees* (1998), a group of residents successfully sued the library to
strike down its policy of installing filters on all computers. This ruling
established Internet use in libraries as a "limited public forum," and
therefore subject to strict scrutiny, an important legal concept. However,
the public forum argument was rejected in the landmark CIPA case,
U.S. v. American Library Association (2003) where Justice Rehnquist's
opinion clearly stated that "Internet access in public libraries is neither
a 'traditional' nor a 'designated' public forum" (p. 8).

While individual librarians in their own settings may differ from this intellectual freedom philosophy, it is generally true that professional librarians will fall on the side of open access to information rather than restricting access through artificial means. This may put them in conflict with officials of the local parent institution: library board, city council, university administration, or in the case of school libraries, principal, teachers, and school board.

As in public libraries, most intellectual freedom issues in school libraries in the twentieth century involved challenges to print publications. As stated by Hopkins (1998), "much of the history for schools in the twentieth century looks at one aspect of intellectual freedom: the removal of materials from school libraries as an infringement of the First Amendment's rights of children" (p. 41). However, soon after she wrote those words, the environment changed. Shirley (2001) states plainly that the question of whether or not to filter Internet access is the most complicated intellectual freedom issue facing school libraries. Leaders in the school library profession are clear in how those challenges should be met. Harriet Selverstone (2001), past President of the American Association of School Librarians and former member of ALA's Intellectual Freedom Committee, states:

> It is our commitment—our responsibility—regardless of our own ethics or morals, to be certain that our constituencies are not withheld information that would be helpful to them. Students need to obtain information for their school research projects, they may need to search for personal health data, and they might even wish to secure information on topics that some people might find inappropriate or offensive ... Living in a democratic society can be burdensome. After all, our society offers choices (of religion, of values, of a wide range of behavior) and respects the right to make each of these

> choices ... Parents still should and must have the right
> and responsibility to decide what THEIR children may
> be exposed to at home, but they should not assume that
> they have the same right and responsibility to impose
> possible restrictions on other people's children. (p.5)

This philosophy and the values of other prominent leaders and their professional associations should be kept in mind during this study as a possible influencing factor in the school library environment. One research question in the study will be to what extent filtering in a school library may infringe on students' First Amendment rights.

Where is the Harm?

A most interesting subset of the recent literature on intellectual freedom involving sexually explicit speech questions the need for protective measures at all. It is simply assumed, in many segments of society, that children suffer harm from exposure to materials considered pornographic. The NRC study, *Youth, Pornography and the Internet* (Thornburgh, 2002), devotes an entire chapter to studying the research base on the impact of sexually explicit material. Empirical research in this area is mostly non-existent due to legal and ethical concerns of Institutional Review Boards across the country. The Committee concludes that "the extant scientific literature does not support a scientific consensus on a claim that exposure to sexually explicit material does—or does not—have a negative impact on children" (p. 362).

Mitchell, Finkelhor, and Wolak (2003) came to the same conclusion about long term effects, but conducted a national survey of youth to examine the question of immediate harm from inadvertent viewing of sexual materials online. They found that 25% of youth using the Internet regularly had at least one unwanted exposure to sexually explicit materials in the past year. Of these, "it is clear from their reactions that the majority of youth regard their personal unwanted exposures as not particularly distressful, little more than nuisances" (p. 350). On the other hand, 24% said they were very or extremely upset by the unwanted exposure.

Marjorie Heins (2001) pushes the question of harm the furthest by challenging the assumption that children must be protected from sexually explicit speech because of the psychological harm it does to them.

> The argument here is not that commercial pornography, mindless media violence, or other dubious forms of entertainment are good for youngsters or should be foisted upon them. Rather, it is that, given the overwhelming difficulty in even defining what it is we want to censor, and the significant costs of censorship to society and to youngsters themselves, we ought to be sure that real, not just symbolic, harm results from youthful pursuit of disapproved pleasures and messages before mandating indecency laws, Internet filters and other restrictive regimes. ... The simultaneous titillation, anxiety and confusion spawned by forbidden speech zones may do more harm than good ... Some older children and adolescents *need* access to information and ideas precisely because they are in the process of becoming functioning members of society and cannot really do so if they are kept in ideological blinders until they are 18. (p. 11-12)

Heins traces the history of censorship back to the days of Plato in ancient Greece, and follows it through the English and then American courts. This is in marked contrast to the Middle Ages, when she bluntly points out that far from being isolated from sex, a child "learned about intercourse by being in the same bed with parents when they did it" (p. 20). However, beginning in the 18th Century and continuing to some extent to the present day, a preoccupation with the supposed evils of masturbation led to an almost fanatical separation of children from all things sexual. In the U.S., court decisions of the Victorian era were characterized by the thinking that obscenity law was designed to prevent immoral litera- ture from falling into the wrong hands (defined as servants, the mentally deficient, women, or minors). Few scholars dared to question the assump- tion that children were irreparably harmed by exposure to explicit sexual materials. Heins ends the book by concluding, as did the Williams Committee in Britain and the Meese Commission in the U.S. that the basic arguments against exposure of pornography to minors are really about morals, not about scientific evidence. While this may be desirable to certain segments of our population, including some parents, schools, and clergy, "underlying our system of free expression is the principle that government officials cannot ban, burden or disfavor speech that they find immoral or offensive ... Citizens decide these matters for themselves" (p. 258). Thus, a research question in the study will consider whether inadvertent contacts with controversial materials harm students.

SUMMARY OF LITERATURE REVIEW

A review of the relevant literature makes it clear that the issue of filtering technology in school libraries is a critical dilemma in today's digital environment. Comprehensive and objective studies of filters reveal ben- efits to users who are concerned that youth may be harmed by access to inappropriate materials on the Internet. This must be balanced by the knowledge that such protectionism may violate students' constitutional rights and may leave them less able to sort out harmful from helpful information on their own in the future. No studies were identified in the literature that described the experiences of students who use the Internet for term paper research in media centers on filtered computers. This proposed study, giving voice to students, teachers, and media specialists, who face these issues on a daily basis, will add to the knowledge base of educators who must be prepared to make and implement Internet filtering decisions.

RESEARCH QUESTIONS

The major research question of this study is: What are the experiences encountered in conducting term paper research using filtered Internet access in a suburban high school media center? Research questions that guide the process of inquiry include:

1) Nature of Internet Use: What is the nature of Internet use for term paper research? Who are the actors? What is the setting? What are the activities? To what extent is there a digital divide in this school?

2) Evaluation of Internet Use with Filters: What sorts of barriers to legitimate information exist with filtered computers? How do students overcome them? To what extent do outside influences (e.g. other people's parents) reach into the day-to-day library research by students?

3) Intellectual Freedom Issues: To what extent does filtering infringe on students' First Amendment rights? Do inadvertent contacts with controversial material harm students?

CHAPTER THREE

METHODOLOGY

The purpose of this project was to describe the experiences of students who conduct term paper research with filtered Internet access in a suburban high school media center. The study involved three main concepts: Internet use in schools, filtering, and intellectual freedom in libraries.

RATIONALE FOR QUALITATIVE METHODOLOGY

Since the purpose of the study was to gather wide-ranging information about student experiences, this most closely matched the qualitative method as described by Creswell (2002), which is used "when the inquirer is interested in exploring and understanding a central phenomenon" (p. 62). In this case, the central phenomenon was term paper research using filtered Internet access. The goal was to explore and understand the implications of using computers with filters, from the point of view of students, teachers and librarians. There were no known studies that explore and describe this phenomenon in detail. The goal was not to prove that filters work or do not work, nor to prove that students are better off with or without filters, but to fill a gap in the literature by studying such library research as it is done.

Qualitative research methods are a relatively recent addition to the landscape of social science research. Denzin and Lincoln (2000) describe the development of qualitative research as a field of inquiry in its own right, beginning with the traditional movement (Malinowski's field experiences in New Guinea in the early 20th Century) to the present, with profound discourse on the ability of the researcher to represent and analyze lived experiences without prejudice. Lincoln and Guba (1985) describe methods of naturalistic inquiry that focus on the participant's view, not the researcher's. "The central perspective of these new approaches is that educational research should consider the participant's view, describe it within a setting or context (e.g. a classroom) and explore the meaning people personally hold for educational issues" (Creswell, 2002, p. 49). To contrast the different approaches: qualitative researchers seek to describe, not measure; they strive to understand, not compare; they focus on the individual, rather than the composite; and they tend to be inclusive, rather than exclusive.

Spradley (1980) says that ethnography is the work of describing a culture. McCombs (1998) gives the following explanation of what ethnographers do:

> Ethnographers listen to and observe in a culture that is of interest to them. They share their observations with the rest of the world in a way that brings those observations alive to the reader, while at the same time providing insights that the natives or inhabitants of that culture might not be aware of because they are so immersed in it. (p. 683)

This is what I have striven to do with the culture of high school students using filtered computers in the media center to conduct research for their term papers.

This study was conducted using qualitative research methods with an emergent design or grounded theory approach. Glaser and Strauss (1967) introduced the concept of grounded theory to mean theories that were identified during data collection, rather than pre-conceived. Others, most notably Charmaz (2000), have refined the concept and added flexibility with a constructivist approach. The basic idea is the same: when rich, descriptive data are gathered and analyzed, patterns will begin to emerge and meaning can be assigned. Thus, the purpose of this study has been deliberately defined in broad terms: to describe the experiences of students who conduct term paper research with filtered Internet access in a suburban high school media center. Conclusions that come from analysis of these experiences rise from the expression of the data.

SITE SELECTION

Lakeside Public School District (pseudonym) was selected as the research site. This site was chosen primarily because of contacts in the district that eased my access. Two school board members were personal and professional acquaintances and the high school librarian expressed interest in the study. The Lakeside school district covers 37 square miles and maintains two high schools, ten elementary schools, and a district-wide vocational and technology center. 96.45% of students in the district graduate from high school. Current demographics are as follows: Caucasian, 92%; African-American, 4.7%; Hispanic, 1.9%; Native American, 0.3%; Asian American, 1.1%.

Lakeside High School has approximately 1,500 students, and has been designated a State Exemplary School and a National Service Learning Leader School. Each classroom is equipped with a telephone, TV/VCR, printer, teacher's computer, and one to three computers for student use. The school sits on a 20-acre campus surrounded by sports fields and modern athletic facilities.

The beautiful, new media center at Lakeside High School is only two years old, having been completely renovated and enlarged during a recent construction project. It holds a well-stocked book and media collection, over 30 computers with Internet access arranged in two class "pods," and ample space for study. The pods were carefully designed to provide full view of student computer screens. The media center is staffed with a professional librarian and one part-time assistant. Over 3,000 students per month visit the facility. There is at least one class using the facilities almost every hour it is open.

The Lakeside district uses the N2H2 "Bess" filtering software produced and sold by Secure Computing. It is not the purpose of this study to evaluate this specific filter. The company claims that Bess is the number one web filtering application for education in over 40% of U.S. schools and libraries. It is paid for by the intermediate school district, but hosted on two local servers by the Lakeside district. Filter administration is done centrally by the district's technology director, whose office is located nearly five miles from the school.

Participant Selection

The method of purposeful sampling (Creswell, 2002) was used to select classes from the school with an assignment to research and write a major term paper. Purposeful sampling allows researchers to intentionally select participants who are likely to provide information rich data. The high school librarian provided the names of nine teachers who typically assign research papers in their classes and who use the media center for their Internet research. All nine teachers were contacted, and two agreed to participate in the study: the Rhetoric teacher and a teacher of General Composition.

Rhetoric is taught to 11th grade students as a pre-requisite for the Advanced Placement Literature course in senior year. Students must obtain a teacher's recommendation in the sophomore year, with confirmation by the English teacher in junior year. Students write eight major papers throughout the year, including an argumentative research paper.

According to the Lakeside curriculum guide, General Composition is recommended for community college bound students. Students from 10th to 12th grades may attend. They write an informative paper, based on a casebook of material provided to them, and may be asked to locate a few additional references on their own.

To recruit students, I attended a classroom session for each group and introduced the research project. I asked interested students to write their home addresses on envelopes that I then mailed to their parents, advising them of the study and giving them the opportunity to prohibit their child's participation by sending back a form in a stamped, self-addressed envelope that I provided. Fifteen students in the Rhetoric class and 13 students in the Basic Composition class provided their home addresses on the envelope. No parents removed their children from the study using the passive, parental exclusion technique described above. Two students in the Basic Composition class were 18-years-old and therefore needed no parental consent. All students signed either assent or consent forms.

ROLE OF THE RESEARCHER

My role as researcher varied throughout the study. Following Spradley (1980), I deliberately engaged in several different participant roles. At times, I was a simple observer, watching students, teachers and librarians interacting during the term paper research process. At other times, I became a participant observer by acting as a troubleshooting assistant to the teacher and librarian in the media center, helping students find Web pages, and answering questions. In this way, I was able to be closer to the experiences of students as they used the filtered computers. I also acted as an interviewer, asking questions of students, teachers and librarians throughout the process, and recording their answers. And finally, I served as an e-mail correspondent with the students, as they sent me the results of their research.

Teachers and librarians tended to treat me as a colleague, trying to understand the behavior of youth. They were also very open with me in an "us" against "them" attitude toward the administration. They either forgot or overlooked the fact that I was a higher education administrator in real life. The students treated me deferentially as an authority figure while in the classroom and media center, calling me "Mrs." and "Ma'am." However, they were much more casual and open in their e-mails, displaying both humor and frustration.

As a professional librarian involved at the national level in intellectual freedom issues, my natural bias is to promote unrestricted access to the Internet. Through use of a researcher's journal, I checked myself on a regular basis to make sure that any bias against filters was not evident to participants in the study. After my final interview with the Basic Composition teacher, she asked me just what my view of the filtering debate was. This reassured me that my bias was not blatantly evident throughout the study.

DATA COLLECTION

I used a combination of data collection techniques: observations, participant observations, semi-structured interviews, focus group interviews, and various kinds of document analysis for my study. In Fall 2002, I had the opportunity to conduct a pilot study that was related to my research by examining the behavior of college students using unfiltered access to the Internet in an undergraduate academic library. Methods included participant observation and semi-structured interviews. This kind of reconnaissance was extremely useful in developing techniques for effective observation and interviewing. I learned that it was possible to identify broad categories of computer use by merely strolling through a computer lab unobtrusively.

Observation of the setting and participants were planned as a way to start data collection. Spradley (1980) describes the difference in degrees of involvement with the activity being studied. Simply observing a class being conducted was a good way to become acclimated to the situation. Participating as a troubleshooter in the media center as students searched the Internet provided closer and richer experiences to describe.

I observed the Basic Composition class once and the Rhetoric Class three times, for one hour each, searching the Internet in the media center, as well as the hour spent in the classroom during recruitment. I took extensive field notes by hand on-site and then word-processed them later for importation into analytical software. I walked around the room, notebook in hand, recording comments, noting where students were searching for information and noting when blocks by the filter occurred. Every 15 minutes, I did site checks, counting how many students were using each of the following sources: databases, Internet, e-mail, library catalog.

I videotaped the final Rhetoric session in the media center in order to gain the rich level of detail that could only be captured live. As Nastasi (Schensul, LeCompte, Nastasi and Borgatti, 1999) describes it, "videotapes permit the consideration of nonverbal behaviors in interpretation of individual or interactive responses" (p. 7). With the level of equipment available to me, it was not possible to discern what individual students were typing or observing on the screen. I reserved the videotape for the trustworthiness technique described by Lincoln and Guba (1985) as referential adequacy, where live episodes captured on tape are held back for later analysis and benchmark testing.

Semi-structured interviews were conducted as the next step in data collection. According to Schensul, Schensul and LeCompte (1999), semi-structured interviews have the flexibility of an unstructured, open-ended interview with the directionality of a survey instrument. I interviewed the librarian and teacher from each class doing term paper research, asking their perspective on students using filtered computers to perform Internet research. Do they observe students encountering barriers? What strategies do they see students using to overcome these barriers? What effect do school filtering policies have on student research? I also interviewed the librarian from the other high school in the district, on the advice of the librarian from Lakeside High School. Finally, I interviewed the technology director for the district, as he was responsible for introducing and implementing the filtering program. In the interviews, I was able to probe for attitudes and opinions on filtered Internet access as well as for interpretations of student behavior.

I conducted hour-long focus group interviews with the students in each class. Schensul (1999) describes focus groups as being a widely accepted means of data collection to study knowledge, attitudes, and beliefs. My belief was that high school students would be willing to share their thoughts if they were in the company of fellow students who were likewise sharing their experiences, and this proved to be the case. In addition, the focus group interviews allowed both on-the-spot corroboration among interviewees and ways for participants to illuminate contrasting viewpoints. The interviews were held during a classroom session after the Internet research phase was complete. They were both audio taped and transcribed. A pizza luncheon during the session encouraged a relaxed atmosphere. Although a script was used, I probed certain responses and in the Rhetoric Class, the teacher jumped in and asked several follow-up questions of her own. In all, I conducted a total of seven, hour-long interviews.

Perhaps the richest form of data came from personal e-mails from students about their search experiences. Students were asked to write journal entries in e-mail format for up to six sessions when they searched for information on the Internet for their term paper. This could be in the media center on filtered computers or at home or elsewhere on unfiltered computers. As an incentive, students who sent at least two e-mails were rewarded with a $10 gift certificate to a local movie theater. Eleven students from Rhetoric and five students from Basic Composition met the requirement and received the reward. I received a total of 49 student e-mails during the course of the study.

The e-mail entries were very rich in descriptive language, revealing frustrations at obstacles and joys at success. The students were very open about their feelings; much more open and descriptive than they were in the media center. One benefit of these writings was that they captured the students' feelings, perceptions, frustrations, and successes while the experience was still fresh in their minds. Most often they wrote from home, after they got back from school. Particularly valuable was their observation of the difference in access between their filtered computer at school and their unfiltered or less restrictive computer at home. It was also very useful when they recorded the actual Web site address of sites that were blocked due to filtering.

A summary of the different kinds of data sets (observations, student journals, individual interviews, focus group interviews, and final term paper analysis) may be found in the grid in Appendix G.

Data Analysis

The process of analyzing qualitative data is generally inductive in form, in that it goes from the particular bit of data (the field note observation, transcribed interview or e-mail text) to emerging themes. This process is as much the art of truth finding as it is science. The process is usually iterative, where data collection and analysis cycle back and forth until a pattern emerges that begins to make sense. Spradley (1980) describes a research cycle that requires constant feedback to give the study direction.

Following Spradley (1980), I first conducted a manual semantic domain analysis by reading through each piece of text and identifying domains of meaning that were grounded in the data (examples include how students feel about being blocked, things teachers say about filters, and ways students get around blocking). I used index cards to record instances in the data where these domains occurred.

Next, I conducted analyses of the word-processed text files (transcribed interviews, field notes from observations, and participant e-mails) using the QSR N6 (NUD*IST) software. I had explored this software in academic courses and it showed great promise for my research. Creswell (2002) describes QSR N6 as offering a "complete toolkit for rapid coding, thorough exploration, and rigorous management and analysis" (p. 262). The redundancy of using both manual and automated analysis techniques served to deepen my analysis considerably. I input the text files into the software and entered the semantic domains from my manual analysis as "nodes." I read the text all over again, this time clicking the nodes whenever I recognized an occurrence of the domain. In this second round, I added a number of occurrences, probably because it was so easy to click, rather than laboriously writing the entry by hand. I also added a number of new nodes that came from deepened familiarity with the data.

The next step was to employ Spradley's (1980) method of taxonomic analysis, which involves identifying the way cultural domains are organized, as shown by related levels. Thus, I sorted the domains into a logical (hierarchical) arrangement. The sense of what was really going on in the media center when students used filtered computers to do their research began to emerge. The beauty of this approach is that the words of the speakers are linked to their nodes of cultural meaning, so that at each step of the classified analysis, the quotations needed to illustrate the point are at hand.

Spradley (1980) advises that the task of the writer is first to understand the cultural meaning through the themes identified in the research and then to communicate them to the reader. I took three different "cuts" to the data to reveal all aspects of their meaning. First, I described profiles of each class, showing their similarities and differences, but also the respective lens of each group. This served to lay out the basic story. Second, I applied semantic domain categories across both classes to focus on particular aspects of the data. Examples included overblocking, underblocking, getting around the filter, etc. This added greatly to the depth of the analysis, letting the words of the speakers illustrate the major points being made. Third, I searched the data for answers to the original research questions, ensuring that the data set was completely exhausted and all aspects of the information were revealed.

TRUSTWORTHINESS

Qualitative research methods in this study followed the interpretive approach to post-structuralist, naturalistic inquiry. Because naturalistic inquiry is criticized by many researchers as lacking the rigor of positivist approaches, Lincoln and Guba (1985) describe a comprehensive set of methods for establishing trustworthiness, or ways of being assured that the findings presented are legitimate and worthy of attention. I used the following methods to earn trustworthiness in this study.

Prolonged Engagement

Prolonged engagement allows sufficient time to learn the culture, test for misinformation and build trust. Observations for this study were conducted over the entire semester, from the first recruitment session to the final focus group interview. Students saw me repeatedly, in the classroom and the media center, as well as corresponding with me by e-mail. In turn, I saw the participants on different days and in different settings to assess whether or not they were telling me what they thought I wanted to hear or what they really felt.

Triangulation

Triangulation is the process of using multiple sources, methods, investigators and theories to verify data. I used different points of view from multiple sources (student, teacher, librarian and administrator) to look at the same issues. In some cases, they served to reinforce each other, and in other cases, distinct interpretations emerged, but in all cases, the data set was enriched and the story became clearer. Triangulation also occurred with different methods (observation, interview and document analysis) used to examine the same behaviors and experiences. In this way, it was possible to see if what a given participant said in an interview was actually borne out by what happened in the media center and vice versa. Triangulation of method also served to deepen the thematic meaning with additional examples of supportive data.

Referential Adequacy

Referential adequacy is the technique of holding aside a live observation on video tape for later analysis and testing for consistency. I viewed the video of the third Rhetoric Class observation in the media center after completing the first draft of the study findings. The video served to confirm the findings that I had already identified, such as blocking of innocuous sites (in this case official government Web sites) and failure to block sexually explicit sites (in this case, how to order pornography online). As previously established, the primary response of the students was annoyance and frustration. No new domains of meaning were evident in this set-aside data, which added to my confidence that the research design and conduct was sound.

Reflexive journal

I kept a reflexive journal from the beginning stages of data collection, which provided the opportunity to check myself for bias, express frustrations, and debate various aspects of the study's methodology with myself. It was here that I could express my values, speculations and personal reflections without the danger of contaminating the field. During several setbacks in site selection and participant recruitment, the journal allowed me to vent and brainstorm for creative solutions. During a six month hiatus in my research due to a job change, I was able to visit the journal occasionally to reassure myself that I would return to the analysis.

LIMITATIONS

The central limitation of this study is its focus on a suburban school with a mostly-white student population from a limited range of social classes. This is a different set of circumstances from urban, rural, and more diverse populations. Although Lakeside teachers complain of budget cuts, the school is, in fact, relatively well-funded, with a beautifully renovated media center and well-maintained computer technology. Most students in the school (and all students in my two classes) have access to computers in their homes as well as in school, although there is a small, but significant Eastern European immigrant population whose children are more likely to rely on school computers. While the findings in this study accurately reflect the situation at Lakeside High School, they may not be interpreted as being valid at schools across America.

SIGNIFICANCE (IMPLICATIONS FOR LEADERSHIP)

Libraries across the country must decide whether and how to filter access to the Internet. The controversies surrounding the Children's Internet Protection Act have brought the issues to the forefront on both the local and national scale. School media centers are in a particularly vulnerable position. On the one hand, they must provide information to young, inquiring minds. On the other hand, media staff feel a responsibility to protect youth who may be more vulnerable than the population at large. Studies on filtering that have appeared in the literature have either been quantitative or prescriptive in nature. As of yet, there has been no published qualitative study of the topic that delves into the multiple realities of what is actually going on when students use filtered computers to search the Internet for research purposes. This study provides heretofore unavailable information to be considered by policy makers when making these difficult decisions. The study reveals that what actually goes on in the classroom and the media center can be quite different from what school administrators think is going on. The voices of students, teachers and librarians may be heard in rich detail as they speak for themselves.

CHAPTER FOUR

INTERNET SEARCHING AT LAKESIDE HIGH

A TALE FROM THE FIELD: JULIE AND THE MPAA

Julie Cho (pseudonym) rushed down the stairs between fifth and sixth periods to get to the media center ahead of her classmates. She wanted to get started on the Internet searching assignment before everyone else came in. She knew that by doing so, she risked earning her reputation of being the nerdiest of nerds, but she didn't care. Her time was precious, couldn't everyone see that? Every day, she got up earlier than any other junior in the class so that she could ride the bus twelve miles to the magnet school program for math and science. She spent three class periods there and then bused twelve miles back to take the last four periods at Lakeside. But because they didn't have all the advanced classes she needed, two of her remaining class hours were spent in on-line distance learning classes from the local community college.

This Rhetoric class was pretty easy, but she liked it because she could choose topics that interested her. The teacher was good about letting her have a freer rein than the other English classes she had had in 9th and 10th grades. Next year would be AP English; she couldn't wait. Today's assignment was Internet searching in the media center to look up references for her research paper. She had chosen to write on the rating system used by the Motion Picture Association of America. She was against it, though practically everyone else in the world supported it. Couldn't they see that it was unfair, inconsistent, and largely unenforceable? Why could she see things so clearly that others could not?

When she got to the media center, she saw that the visiting doctoral student was there, ready to take notes on their class. I hope she doesn't slow me down, Julie thought. She told us in class that she was interested in the filter that the school used. Now there was a useless idea. Julie had experienced being blocked by the filter for many other papers; she wondered what it would do with the MPAA topic. She booted up the computer while the other kids were still filing in and talking. She had never liked the Vivisimo meta-search engine selected by the school, but whatever. She typed in "MPAA ratings" and got the usual cluster of results. She clicked the first one, BLOCKED. Oh no. She clicked the next cluster heading. BLOCKED. Come on. She clicked all the remaining cluster headings and couldn't follow a single link. What is going on? They can't all be pornographic! Then the computer said she had to log out and log back on again because there were too many blocks. For crying out loud! This time after booting up, she remembered a trick another students told her about and went to Alta Vista instead. Presto. The same search went through and she could at least get through to the mpaa. org site. But when she went to follow the link, she got blocked again, probably because it said "explicit sexual content" on the page. But that was only the definition being used; there was nothing on the page that looked bad. Now I've wasted ten minutes and got nowhere. I don't even have one reference and I need twenty. She could hear her classmates squealing when they got blocked as well. And that doctoral student kept wandering around taking notes, smiling to herself. What does she want? Does she want us to get blocked or not? Julie decided to forget trying to search the Internet at school. She should have known better. She usually did her Web searching at home because she could search more freely there. The computers here just wasted her time and she didn't have time to waste. After school she had band practice and then had to be back again at six o'clock for a concert. For the rest of the time in the media center, she searched the indexing databases that the school librarian had told them about. For some reason, the filter didn't seem to interfere as much with them. She got five good articles printed off from sources like the *Christian Science Monitor* and *The New York Times* before her teacher told the class to stop. She reminded them to send an e-mail to the doctoral student lady describing their experiences at the media center. Julie was starting to think that the school's filter was just as ineffective as the MPAA rating system. When adults try to protect kids from things they consider dangerous, sometimes they go too far. Kids can handle a lot more than adults think they can. Well, maybe not little kids, but the kids in her class were out there *doing* the things that the adults didn't want them to see pictures of. It was all such a waste of time.

FINDINGS

In this chapter, I describe the findings of the project that result from analysis of qualitative data. The broad purpose of the study was to describe the experiences of students who conduct term paper research with filtered Internet access in a suburban high school media center. Methods used to collect data on these experiences included participant observation of classroom and media center activities, semi-structured interviews of students, teachers, librarians, and the district technology administrator, focus group interviews of each class of students, and e-mailed journal entries from the students after each research session in the media center.

Narrative analysis performed both manually using the methods described by Spradley (1980), and from automated data analysis using QSR N6, revealed broad categories of findings from the rich, descriptive data. Analysis is organized first by a description of each class, then by cross-class semantic domain analysis, and finally by using the data to answer the research questions posed in the study.

Class Profiles

Rhetoric Class

The Rhetoric class was well-prepared for their Internet searching sessions in the media center. The Rhetoric teacher had over 30 years experience at this school and had collaborated often with the librarian on research assignments. The teacher made sure that the librarian had visited their classroom twice before they actually went to the media center to begin searching. The librarian lectured the students on choosing a topic, finding reliable, unbiased Internet sources for their papers, differentiating between databases of periodical literature and Web sites, and introducing them to the concept of Boolean logic. She returned to the class a second time and gave students feedback on the sources they had found on their own. As the Rhetoric teacher said:

> Initially, all they want to do is a Google search. The hardest part for them is sorting through information on what is reliable. But the librarian worked with them on this. She came into class and showed them how to get reliable sources. Even the most sophisticated students have trouble with this.

When the Rhetoric students got to the media center for the first of three visits, they showed remarkable restraint in using the Internet at first, and most of them first tried to find the two book sources that were required for the assignment. They needed quite a bit of help in using the online catalog and then finding the books on the shelf, which were arranged in the Dewey Decimal system.

When they did begin Internet searching, blocking from the filter started right away. One girl was blocked from www.cannabis.com and many other sites while researching the legalization of marijuana for medicinal purposes. She said, "I know that my topic is about a drug, but given that the topic is on the medicinal uses of the drug, I was a little angry at the amount of sites that were blocked." A boy was blocked at the www.ncaa.org site while searching for information on compensating college athletes. He had come across a page in the site that talked about "cheating." Another girl had chosen the topic of book banning in schools and was repeatedly blocked when using the terms "corruption" and "banned." The girl who was writing on smoking bans in restaurants was blocked by the term "smoking bans." The girl who had the most trouble with being blocked had chosen to write on the Motion Picture Association of America rating system.

> Yesterday, when we were searching in the library for our research project, I was blocked a series of times. I was blocked around 10 or 11 times trying to get to certain Web sites that appeared to be completely legitimate to me. Nothing on the sites seemed to be wrong or inappropriate. I went to many of the sites when I got home and there was nothing on the Web sites that should have been blocked. All the Web sites gave me were some very good information on the topic.

The students in the Rhetoric Class had been trained on using databases that indexed articles in newspapers and periodicals, as well as the Web. A number of them learned quickly that there was little blocking when searching the databases but that blocking was much more frequent when searching the Web. The student researching smoking bans in restaurants said, "I only went to sites through InfoTrac (online periodical database) today so there were not any sites or areas that were restricted to me." The girl studying medicinal purposes of marijuana reported,

> I was not able to go on to a number of Web sites. I was able to get on sites that were under MEL (set of Michigan Research Library databases made available through state funding); however when I searched under Google, nine times out of ten I was not allowed on the site.

Another girl offered, "Today I searched the databases through MEL and went into different Web sites on religion in school and prayer in school, those are what I typed in. Every Web site I went to let me in, but there were not many results."

Rhetoric students also recognized that they were not likely to get blocked if they were researching non-controversial topics. A girl writing on school dress codes said,

> As a result of being in the school media center for three days, I have not had one problem getting any of the necessary information. I think this is because I am doing my paper on school uniforms and that topic does not have any controversial key words that would cause a filter to block out information.

Another girl doing research on the USA PATRIOT ACT wrote, "I'm not meeting a lot of problems with the filters because my topic doesn't involve a lot of words that would be blocked."

Basic Composition Class

Students in the Basic Composition class were notably less prepared and less sophisticated in their searching. The teacher had only been at the school three years and preferred an independent approach to teaching.

Although the librarian had repeatedly offered to meet with the class before their visit to the media center, the teacher declined. When I asked what preparation the students were given before they went to the media center to search for information, the teacher said, "Pre-existing knowledge is their preparation." Since students in this class had already been given a casebook of sources they were to use in their papers on the topic of "mental institutions," they only needed to find three additional references. There was no requirement to use print resources, such as books. On their first of two trips to the media center, the teacher instructed them:

> Based on your outline, you are here to fill in the holes. What you want to do is break down your categories, like putting things in your drawers. The top drawer is how to start your paper. Then you might have a junk drawer, that's the best way I've figured out how to describe it.

Since the students did not know anything about searching databases, they immediately started searching the Web and immediately started getting blocked. Typically, they would type a word or phrase such as "mental institutions" into the search engine's text box or sometimes directly into the Web address box. These random results would take them to bulletin board sites (www.voy.com and www.unsolvedmysteries.com) or online publishers (www.suite101.com) that would block them if anything on the page violated the filter. One girl accessing www.suite101.com said, "This site sounded extremely informational, helping with the abuse topic, but the summary about the information said 'sexual abuse' in it, not allowing me on it." Since almost all the students used the same unsophisticated technique and limited themselves to the first page of results from the search engine, most of them were blocked on these same sites. One student said, "Today I got a lot of information from the sites. But 'Mental Institutions' is very hard to research because of its limited resources on the net. But I was blocked from a few sites." It struck me that a student would think that there was very little information on the Internet about mental institutions.

Central Issues for Filtered Internet Use

Several key issues arose from the data surrounding the use of filtered computers for Internet research. Multiple instances occurred in each category across both classes of students.

Overblocking

Overblocking occurs when an appropriate site is mistakenly deemed inappropriate and blocked from the user. According to the director of technology for the Lakeside school district, the N2H2 Bess filter is used at the default setting level, although staff may adjust the settings at their discretion. The standard content categories that are blocked are:

Adults Only
Alcohol
Chat
Drugs (but not the subcategory Drug Education)
Jokes
Lingerie

In the two years since this particular filter has been in operation, district officials have closed access to ten individual Web sites and opened access to nine. Among the blocked sites are:

www.google.com/images
www.blackplanet.com
www.surpasssupport.com
www.livejournal.com
www.download.com

The sites that have been opened upon request include:

www.yahooligans.com
www.autotrader.com
www.schoolnotes.com

In actual practice, students experienced blocking for many sites that could be explained by the standard blocked categories above, but they also experienced blocking from words, phrases or Web sites not easily explained (the phenomenon of overblocking). These included:

www.ncaa.org
www.vivisimo.com - subcategories
www.ama.org
www.mpaa.org

Sometimes when a seemingly innocuous site caused a block, it was due to a word or phrase on the page. The girl researching the MPAA ratings system observed,

> It's very frustrating to not be able to get into certain sites that are really worth my time. A lot of those sites that I couldn't get into on the school computer gave me various critical information, such as the reasons why people are against the MPAA rating system. I think that the filtering system for the school is too strict. The sites were probably blocked due to the fact that they had a few words such as 'explicit sexual content' on the site. However, there was nothing on the site that was inappropriate for students.

I asked the students and teachers if they ever considered asking to have the administration remove the block so they could get to the site they needed to visit. One teacher was adamant that she had never heard of this possibility, saying:

> It's never been explained to me that we could do it, ask to have a site unblocked. The teachers don't know that. It's never been in the *Technology News*. It's never been in any policy I have ever read. Besides, it would take too long. We only had three days to do our research.

Only two individuals, one teacher and one student, were aware of this procedure even though the screen that popped up when a block occurred gave detailed information on what to do.

FIGURE 1.   Screen Shot of Blocking Message

The student told of her experience in trying to get a site unblocked,

> Once I wanted to get to a site, so I signed up at the counseling office, but I couldn't get called down. You never get called down for anything. It's impossible. I just figured I would never get the chance to change it. It would never actually happen.

The teacher told a similar, though more successful, story:

> I am blocked personally almost daily. I would like to see the rules and would like to find out why certain things are blocked. I have done the policy exception thing. One day I tried to get to Spark notes and found it was blocked. When I asked why, they said they equated it with cheating. I got it unblocked, but it took two days.

One student questioned the entire exception policy on principle, "But why should you have to go out of your way to get to something that is harmless anyway? It is easier to open violent games, which are not blocked at all, than to get to something legitimate."

The technology director, however, had a much different view of what is actually happening in the schools, "The procedure is adequate to open sites up ... There are very few, if any, requests for site openings."

Underblocking

Even though it happened much less frequently than overblocking, students also experienced underblocking, that is, the filter failed to block sites that actually contained objectionable material in the categories it tried to block. When this happened, students became indignant. One blurted out in the media center, "Just what I need, ten reasons to be a transsexual!" Another girl said, "Why is crackwalker2tripod.com not blocked when my medicinal sites are blocked? It shows how to grow marijuana!" The MPAA girl said, "I got through to a site that showed how to order porn movies, but all the other blockings were good sites that should have been let through." Another day, the same student said:

> I did some research at home and the blocker at my house actually
> blocks a few of the inappropriate sites that were not blocked at
> school, such as the ordering porn from cable companies. That's
> interesting, considering the school SHOULD be blocking that
> information but isn't. Yet my home blocker blocks it, and it's
> set on a low setting.

The students observed that the school's filter seemed to be inconsistent in what it blocked. One complained,

> The blocking system at the school seems to be very inaccurate and seems to change every ten minutes. One site that is blocked will be blocked but ten minutes later it changes and is not blocked anymore. The system also lets some inappropriate sites through as a few of my other classmates found out.

Getting Around the Filter

Students were very upfront about the fact that they found a number of ways to get around the filter to avoid blocking. One student unabashedly explained, "I found a way around the blocking system and you can get into any sites you want if you go about it the right way. There is a way to cheat the system!" Methods to fool the filter include: using a different search engine to follow direct links to the site, use of the "refresh" button, page translators, and a change in terminology.

One of the most common ways to get around the filter is simply to go home and repeat the search on one's home computer.

> I've done that multiple times. Lots of blocked sites at school
> were perfectly legitimate. Some were government sites and
> all had good information and were legitimate. PDF files were all
> blocked at school so I had to go home to get to them.

Another student agreed:

> Once I got home on Friday I went to my computer and tried
> the same sites that had been blocked at school. None of those
> sites that were blocked were inappropriate and actually, some
> of the sites were inappropriate but not blocked on the computer
> at school. The system seems to be very unsure of what it is
> supposed to block and what it is not supposed to block.

How Students Feel about Blocking

When students were asked how they feel about the experience of having
material blocked by the filter, their most common responses were
"frustrated," "annoyed," or "angry." A sampling of responses: "It's
very frustrating to not be able to get into certain sites that are really
worth my time." "It was very frustrating on Friday when all the sites
that came up on the database Vivisimo were blocked." "I was a little
angry at the amount of sites that were blocked." "I'm wondering if
there are so many other useful and helpful Web sites out there that,
because of our school's filters, I'm not able to get to. That makes me
very frustrated." "It's incredibly annoying that I can't get to information sites but ads about some pill that show a man and a woman in each
other's arms are allowed to pop up on me." "It is frustrating to find it
blocked, you have to use a site you are not used to, to get around it."
Perhaps one student said it best, "Well, yet again the filters decided not
to like me."

Some students expressed dismay that the school did not trust
them to go unfiltered. "The school holds us back enough as it is. It's
the whole equality thing. Not wanting anyone to do it. We shouldn't
be held back." "It's not like we're not mature enough not to close
it out if something comes up." "It's not fair ... we can handle this
stuff."

Overall Assessment of the Filter

Among those who contributed to the survey, the district technology director alone thought that the filter was doing its job effectively. "I believe N2H2 is maintaining an appropriate balance between instructional content and content that is deemed inappropriate by the teaching staff." What his statement actually revealed was how much out of touch he was with what was really going on in the schools.

The librarians working in the schools had a much different view. The librarian who had been there before filters were installed said, "I told them at the outset that I thought that Bess (filter name) didn't work." Later, she went on to say:

> I don't think filters work in general. The real filter in education is the teacher. You need to be there, you need the hands on ... Now I can say a filter doesn't work. No, I'm the one who is ultimately responsible. If a filter failed and there's a bad site, then I'm the second filter.

The librarian at the other high school in the district offered a more philosophical view:

> In most cases, the kind of research the kids do is not affected by the filtering policy ... We don't have cases where the kids can't finish their assignment unless I call the Help Desk. And then they can get it from home, they can get anything they want there. That's not an issue ... I'm more concerned from a censor point of view you could have an institution that didn't want them to see certain points of view.

The Basic Composition teacher was very opposed to filtering at the high school level:

> I find it very off-putting to students ... Appropriate sites are blocked. Last year we were doing research on the homeless

and those kids couldn't find anything because all drug names were blocked. Same thing happened this year with the mental institutions theme ... At the high school level, I feel they should be monitored on an individual level. I am generally opposed to mass solutions. It doesn't teach them how to use judgment. I haven't seen a big porn problem among students. It just isn't there. Reality is now the Web address. Putting a lock on it doesn't help. They have to learn to deal with it, because it's there. I am totally opposed to filtering in a public library or university setting.

The teacher of the Rhetoric class thought there should have been more input sought from teachers before the filters were put in place:

Teachers have never been asked what they thought about filters or how they should be used ... I think it frustrates students, but it may not be prohibitive. I don't really recall any student who had to abandon a topic because of it. The student who was writing on censorship of films, the rating system, had a lot of difficulty and I felt that was the filtering system. She wasn't doing anything wrong, but the filter kept blocking her.

Students in each class were specifically asked during the focus group interview, "Overall, do you think the school filtering policy helps you in your work or hinders you? Explain." The teacher in the Rhetoric Class required each participating student to take a position on this and state reasons. Their responses were very clear:

"Hinders: I don't see how it could help. I mean you can hear all kinds of bad things in the hall, but then you can't go on the Internet. It's a double standard and I don't think it helps at all."

"Helps: I think it helps. It filters out the things you don't need and the bad stuff."

"Hinders: I was looking for a picture of a skin disease in Anatomy class and I couldn't get any picture at all, and it wasn't anything bad. I had to go home to get a picture for my presentation."

"Hinders: even if you're still in a Google search, you can't access them, you have to go back, it doesn't matter where you saw it. It's so annoying."

"Hinders: Even though there is a point that they have the filters in high school because 99% of the kids in school are too immature to handle that kind of thing. But for kids like us, when we're trying to do research, it's not fair to us to go to all the trouble to go home or to another library to look things up just because the kids are too immature to deal with it. We can handle this stuff."

"Hinders: it's pointless; there are always teachers and adults around anyway if we're looking at something we're not supposed to be looking at. We wouldn't be able to do it for long, or even at all, so therefore, why even have it if it's causing so many problems?"

"Hinders: the blocked sites are not going to be bad, even the one on marijuana is not harmful."

"Hinders: bad sites still come up anyway in all our searches. Obviously, we're gonna go home and use those same sites and same search engines. So there's no point in doing it double time."

"Hinders: my topic was smoking and it gave me biased results. There were no good sites to support it, which I needed. I know the school doesn't want to give us sites that say smoking is good for you, but I had to present both sides."

"Hinders: overall, even though I didn't have any problems in mine, I think it's a totally ineffective system."

"Hinders: I didn't have any problems with my term paper, but I don't think it helps. My anatomy class was hard to do, and I couldn't get any pictures, and besides, some people don't have access at home. Even when my computer was broke at home I had to come here to get it."

"Hinders: it definitely hurts, because if there is a site that's blocked, more than likely people will find a way around it anyway. So the system is basically useless. It blocks sites that shouldn't be blocked and doesn't block sites that should be blocked, so it's very inaccurate as to what it's supposed to be blocked."

"Hinders: how could anything that restricts information be helpful with research? I mean, that is what my topic is all about: book banning. Restricting information like that is not going to help you; it's just going to hurt you."

Thus, twelve out of the thirteen Rhetoric students present said that filtering hindered their ability to conduct research for their term paper. It is possible that peer pressure influenced the students to agree with those who spoke before them, but from the personal examples that they gave from their own experiences, they are credible in their responses.

The Basic Composition class, though lacking the intellectual status of the Rhetoric class, gave an impressively balanced, nuanced response. They were asked the same question, "Overall, do you think the school filtering policy helps you in your work or hinders you? Explain." The teacher did not require them to state an individual position, but as the interviewer, I nodded to each participant, giving them the opportunity to respond.

"It gets in the way. It's useful, but it gets in the way."

"It's a pain. Truly, you are under surveillance in school all the time anyway, why do you need the filter?"

"It hasn't helped at all. It takes a lot longer to do research–like ten minutes instead of two."

"It's a pain, but it's necessary because of other immature people, but they could take it down a notch to allow the regular stuff to be unblocked."

"I feel the same way. It takes longer, but a little bit of filtering is good."

"I don't mind it because I can always use my computer at home."

"Sometimes it is in the way, but if you really want to look at something, you can get around it."

"It's a pain, but some people are bad apples and they make everyone suffer."

"It hurts us. It takes forever to find stuff. The immature people get caught anyway."

"It's not bad or good. There is always a way around it."

"It's a nuisance, but we do need a filter of some kind. Sites open up even if you don't click on them."

"It's annoying, but necessary because of the bad stuff."

In this class, three students gave entirely negative responses, stating that the filter hindered them. One student gave a positive response to the filter, saying she could always use her home computer. Eight students qualified their answers by saying that the filter had negative points but overall it was necessary and it was possible to get around it, anyway. Again, one could speculate that peer pressure was at work and once an "established answer" was given, there was a temptation to replicate it.

Interestingly, students in both classes gave the distinct impression that while they themselves could handle controversial material without a filter, if it was necessary at all, it was because of "other, immature" students in school. The Rhetoric class was distinctly judgmental about General Composition students: "This is nothing against the other kids in school because they're not in Rhetoric, but in General Comp, they only play around in school. They go home and do their own search anyway." "Lots of General Comp classes don't go down to the library anyway because they know they're going to misbehave." "Chances are they're not even going to have to need it, so why should we be penalized?"

The Basic Composition class likewise felt that it must be other students who were not mature enough to go without filtering, "It's a pain, but it's necessary because of other immature people." "It's a pain, but some people are bad apples and they make everyone suffer." "It hurts us. It takes forever to find stuff. The immature people get caught anyway."

Alternate Solutions

Both classes of students offered many alternate solutions to the problem that caused the school to impose filters on them. The Rhetoric class felt particularly strongly about pop-up blockers. In the Rhetoric focus group, one girl said "It might do better to get a pop-up blocker. That would solve almost everything." This generated nearly universal agreement. Another girl offered, "If teachers would take responsibility and walk around and see what kids are looking at, that would take care of it. It depends on the teacher." Another student favored a profiling system:

> Find a way to get the server fixed so that certain students aren't on the blockers. Certain classes could use a different configuration to not be blocked – it could be by logon. So if you're in a more advanced class that needs research like Rhetoric or Anatomy then you're going to need all the resources. It could be by individual logon or by class.

The Basic Composition class was equally creative, if not more so, in their brainstorming of alternate solutions. They agreed about the pop-ups:

"It is the pop-ups that are bad; some are blocked, some are not. It's mostly like dating sites, not hard pornography."

"Every teacher could get a certain password to turn the filter off to use in a class."

"It could be programmed to have a special computer without the filter and the teacher could stay with you after school."

"They could change the level from middle school to high school. The filter shouldn't be the same for different age levels."

"There could be a trial period without the filter to see if any harm would come from it."

"They could ease up on the filter so that it would just block porn and not the regular stuff."

Students had many good ideas on how to manage the situation, but sadly, they were never asked for input by their school.

Answers to Research Questions

Another way I analyzed the data was to probe for answers to the original research questions in the rich narrative text provided by the participants. Thus, the three main categories of research questions were systematically examined: 1) Nature of Internet Use, 2) Evaluation of Internet Use with Filters, and 3) Intellectual Freedom Issues.

Nature of Internet Use

What is the nature of Internet use for term paper research? The nature of Internet use varied considerably with the two different classes. The Rhetoric class prepared well in advance for their Internet searching sessions in the media center. The school librarian had visited the class twice to give them guidance in selecting and narrowing a topic and then in Boolean search techniques. They knew the difference between Web sites and scholarly periodical literature. They were very cautious about using what their teacher called "biased" sites. They had an assignment to begin finding sources for their paper and then had the librarian critique those sources. When they began searching, they quickly learned that blocking was much more likely to occur when they used the Web, rather than in periodical databases provided by the school. They recognized that the subject matter of their chosen topic had much to do with the likelihood of being blocked, namely, that topics on controversial subjects like book banning or film rating systems were much more likely to be blocked than school uniforms or the Electoral College.

The Basic Composition class had only "pre-existing knowledge" as their preparation for Internet searching. They did not have to worry about selecting and narrowing a topic, since their topic of "Today's Mental Institutions" was already defined. However, they were allowed some selectivity in emphasizing one aspect over the other. Those who chose to emphasize sub-topics such as "abuse" encountered more blocking than others. They only had to find three sources in addition to the forty-eight page casebook that had been provided for them. When they were told to start searching, nearly all typed "mental institutions" into the search window of their chosen search engine and when they started clicking on the search results, they reported the same blocks.

Who are the actors? The students of the Rhetoric and Basic Composition classes were the primary actors in this study. Each class had a distinct character. The Rhetoric students are the "cream of the crop," as their teacher calls them, and they know it. They are the students who will go on to first-rate universities and have a chance to use and improve on the skills that they learn in Rhetoric. They will write many term papers in the future and will be glad for the training given to them in this exercise. They understand that the kind of Internet surfing they do in their leisure time is far different from the kind of academic searching that is required for serious course work. They have different needs from the Basic Comp students. They went to great lengths to explain how busy they are and therefore, how the school should not "hold them back." One student said, "We don't get too much time to get everything done. Kids in the advanced classes are usually busy with other things like band, clubs, sports. Blocking takes time." Another student simply said, "Our time is precious."

The Basic Composition students were clearly less gifted in their use of language and were less strongly motivated. Their e-mails and answers to written and verbal questions were always shorter than their Rhetoric counterparts. Their teacher had to constantly cajole and remind them to meet basic commitments in the class. However, when they did participate, they proved to be perceptive and creative in their own right. They shared a confidence identical to the more advanced Rhetoric students that they were perfectly capable of handling the real world on its own terms and did not really need the filter that was mandated by the school. Both groups of students, however, recognized that there might be "other" students in the school, less mature than they, who would need the filter to stay in line and out of trouble. I did not meet any of those students. I wonder if they exist.

Besides the students, teachers and librarians proved to be key actors as well. The teachers in the two classes varied dramatically in their approach to the term paper assignment. The Rhetoric teacher's advance preparation assignments definitely gave these students an advantage when it came time to perform actual research on the Internet. This teacher gave the librarian adequate time to help the students with sophisticated searching techniques. The librarian was effectively shut out of the Basic Composition experience, due to that teacher's preferences. These students were left on their own to search as they would search at home for leisure activities.

What is the setting? Lakeside High School is a middle-class, suburban, Midwestern high school with approximately 1500 students in four grades. It was built in the late 1950's and has been continuously updated and expanded. The latest expansion included a second gymnasium, a swimming pool and a completely new media center with extensive Internet access. Demographics show that the school district is 92% white. All students in both the Rhetoric and Basic Composition classes reported that they have computer access at home, which means that they are experienced Internet users and also means that the school media center is not their sole source of access.

What are the activities? Observation of students in the classroom revealed a variety of activities. Students in both classes were relaxed, open, and friendly with their teachers and with me, as an interested observer. They were seen to talk to each other before and during class, raise their hands, answer questions, and ask questions of their own. They willingly participated in the class focus group as part of a regular class session.

In the media center, behavior diverged between the two classes. Rhetoric students were required to use at least two print sources, so they had to learn to use the online catalog and figure out the Dewey Decimal system to find a book on the shelf. Rhetoric students made much more use of the periodical databases provided by the school. I performed activity checks every 15 minutes during each observation. Rhetoric students used periodical databases 72% of the time, Internet searching 10%, and e-mail (required in the assignment) 18%. In contrast, Basic Composition students performed general Internet searching almost exclusively, 98% of the time and e-mail only 2%. They were not observed to use the periodical databases available to them at all, which may not be surprising, considering no one showed them how to find them or how to use them.

To what extent is there a digital divide in the school? Defining "digital divide" as the difference in access to digital information that separates the information-rich from the information-poor, I observed no evidence of a digital divide at Lakeside High School. This is attributed primarily to the fact that every student in both classes had computer access at home, as well as at school. This may not be surprising, given the fact that the district is 92% white and considered to be in the middle to upper-middle economic class. If the school's filter blocked them during class, they went home and went to the same site, unblocked, to get the information. Only one student mentioned that her home computer had a filter and she specifically said that she was able to access harmless sites that the school computer erroneously blocked. Because there was no digital divide, one data source did not prove to be as fruitful as I had anticipated. The term papers written by the students did not demonstrate a lack of access to relevant information because students used their home computers to fill in the gap created by the filtered computers at school.

What is surprising is that perceptive individuals in both classes recognized the *potential* for a digital divide in theoretical cases where students did not have computers at home. In the Rhetoric class focus group, one girl brought this up on her own, in answer to my final, generic question, "Is there anything else you can think of that might help me in this study?" She said,

> For kids that don't have Internet access or computer access at home, it's discrimination. They are usually low income. I just wrote a paper about not being able to be a part of certain things and it's not fair. It usually depends on how much funding a school gets and since they are a branch of government, they are not allowing them to be a part of what they could be.

In the Basic Composition class, I asked a follow-up probe to the "help or hinder" question, "Tell me how you feel about this: what if you were a kid who didn't have a computer at home and could only get your information from the school library or public library that had filters?" A very perceptive girl in the class immediately saw the significance of this and said, "That would be bad because kids like that don't get the whole story–they only get what the filter will let through." It is very impressive that these teenagers could see through to the long-term societal consequences of poverty and an over-protective government more than their teachers and administrators, who never expressed the same concern throughout the course of the study. It gives credence to the students' belief that they are mature enough to handle the occasional inappropriate site in exchange for open access to information.

Evaluation of Internet use with Filters

What sorts of barriers to legitimate information exist with filtered computers? As documented in the "Overblocking" section, the data show that the filter used by the school to block harmful Web sites also served as a barrier to legitimate information. The students who were researching topics that might be considered controversial, such as legalization of marijuana for medicinal purposes or book banning in schools, experienced the most over-blocking. The student who experienced the most blocking did her paper on the film rating system of the Motion Picture Association of America. She stated her case clearly:

> The sites that were blocked actually were reputable sites that would have been useful for my research, however, I could not get to them due to a few articles that discussed pornography and how nudity in movies should be rated. It wasn't anything graphic; it just simply stated the fact that that is a problem.

How do students overcome these barriers? Students demonstrated several ways to overcome the barrier of being blocked from legitimate sites. The most common method was simply to go home and access the site there. A Rhetoric student with the topic of juvenile punishment reported in her e-mail journal entry,

> I was searching through the *USA Today* Web site and I clicked a link to get to a certain document about the legislature passed on my topic. BUT I WAS BLOCKED! DUN DUN DUN!... I plan to access the site I was blocked from at school and see if it has any relevance... [Two days later, she wrote]... I wanted to let you know I reached that site at my house and I am able to use it on my term paper and will be doing that.

Students identified several other methods of overcoming the blocking barrier. One was to use a different search engine than Vivisimo, which was listed on the library's Web site under "Search the Internet". One student said, "AltaVista is the main way to get around anything here." Another agreed, "There's a way to get around the blocks, just use AltaVista." The Basic Composition teacher heard this and said, "I know, four to five students have told me. It's just that I don't endorse my students acting illegally!" Another method was simply to change terminology. For example, a student was blocked when using the term "drugs", but was not blocked when changing it to "substance abuse." Students in both classes learned that blocks could be avoided by using a page translator,

> The funny thing about filters is that one can get around them by going through a page that translates Web sites into other languages. The site comes up under the translator's site and is therefore displayed. It is, however, not possible to send any information from a translated page because it's thrown off by the translation.

That student's teacher sighed and said, "Students taught me that one, I didn't know it on my own."

To what extent do outside influences reach into the day-to-day library research of students? Callister and Burbules (2003) point out that when a school district says it is protecting children by using filters, the real intent may be to protect teachers and administrators from unpleasant consequences. Rather than go through the difficult, and sometimes embarrassing, process of teaching students to distinguish between appropriate and inappropriate sites, filters provide an easy way out.

> Filters are a way of protecting teachers from the upsetting nuisance of dealing with unpleasant or controversial topics in the classroom. Filters are a way of protecting school administrators from having angry phone calls (even lawsuits) from parents concerned over occasional instances where students go to "bad" places on the Internet. Filters are a way for adults generally to avoid the hassle of dealing with instances of student misconduct, after the fact, by attempting to forestall the act before it ever occurs. (p. 3)

Both teachers and students recognized that it was likely due to outside influences (other people's parents) that the school installed filters in the first place, rather than input from librarians, teachers, or students. The technology administrator said this up front, "We had some students bring up inappropriate sites and parents complained." The Rhetoric teacher said, "I believe some of it is 'political correctness'–pressure from parents." One of the students showed a fairly high degree of sophistication when she philosophically recognized that it was community pressure that brought about the filters:

> But as a school, you can't have this stuff popping up. I can see it from their point of view. That looks bad to the community and makes the school look bad. But they need to find a more effective way.

Another student was less patient with the idea that she was being judged by others according to the information that she used in the library, "If someone looked at my library record, I've read books on Hitler. Does that mean they think I'm a Nazi?"

Gutmann (1987) states:

> A democratic state recognizes the value of parental education in perpetuating particular conceptions of the good life, ... recognizes the value of professional author- ity in enabling children to appreciate and to evaluate ways of life other than those favored by their families, ... [and] recognizes the value of political education in predisposing children to accept those ways of life that are consistent with sharing the rights and responsibili- ties of citizenship in a democratic society. (p. 42)

This then suggests that Lakeside administrators did an inadequate job of taking into account all of these genuine stakeholders, responding rather to a small set of parents who had visions of the good life that were not shared by all parents. Our government has implemented a strategy to appreciate that youth are not adults and there can be limits on their intellectual freedom, but it is important for school officials to understand that the fine points do matter, and having an effective "out" is essential to the whole notion of filtering being acceptable. Further, Lakeside provided no way to continue the deliberation about this decision or to accommodate those parents who do not have this narrower sense of what students should access. In fact, these conservative parents have been given too much authority and there has been no way to incorporate balance among differing versions of a good life. Balance lost out here.

Intellectual Freedom Issues

To what extent does filtering infringe on students' First Amendment rights? It is well established in the courts that students have First Amendment rights (*Board of Education, Island Trees Union Free School District No. 26 v. Pico,* 1982), although they can be different from those of adults. From the data provided above, it is clear that the high school students at Lakeside High School were prevented by their school's filter from accessing what in any other setting would be considered constitutionally protected speech. However, even in *Pico,* the Court's opinion made clear that while school library books may not be removed because officials disagreed with the ideas expressed in the books, had the books been found educationally unsuitable or "pervasively vulgar," the removal decisions would have been ruled constitutional. Writing before the Supreme Court ruled in CIPA, Willard (2002) suggested that the use of commercial Internet filtering software in schools would ultimately be found to be unconstitutionally restrictive of student access to the Internet. However, because of the Supreme Court's surprisingly conservative ruling in the recent CIPA case (*U.S. v. American Library Association,* 2003), it is highly unlikely that any court would rule a filter used by schools to keep children safe unconstitutional. The deciding factor in weighing the benefits against potential harm for public library patrons in CIPA was the supposed capability to turn the filter off. Since the Lakeside School District has an established policy and procedure to request reinstatement of blocked Web sites, the fact that it does not work in an effective or timely way is not likely to be convincing to the courts. The Court in CIPA did not require the filter to be perfect, only well-intentioned.

Do inadvertent contacts with controversial material harm students? The ostensible reason for installing filters in schools is to protect children from harm. Most reasonable people would agree that protecting children from harm is a reasonable goal. But what constitutes harm? Is embarrassment considered harmful? Callister and Burbules (2003) suggest that what is often judged harmful is actually what makes *adults* feel uncomfortable. Web sites may be inappropriate for high school aged students, but does that make them harmful? Further, they imply that the pop-up ads that the Lakeside students found so irritating may actually do more harm in the long run through their emphasis on corporate marketing than a brief glimpse of naked breasts. In the literature of the topic, Marjorie Heins (2001) goes the furthest in questioning what actual harm takes place when children are exposed to materials considered pornographic. She posits, 'We ought to be sure that real, not just symbolic, harm results from youthful pursuit of disapproved pleasures and messages before mandating decency laws, Internet filters and other restrictive regimes" (p.11).

Students in both classes treated the accidental exposure to inappropriate sites fairly casually. They used words such as "stupid," and "no big deal." When asked, "Have you ever come across a controversial Web site by accident? If so, how did you feel about that?" One student said, "It's not that big of a deal. You just press 'Back' and go about your business." Another said, "Most of it is stuff we've seen before." Some students admitted to embarrassment, "One time something came up by accident at home and my dad happened to walk in and said, 'What are you looking at?' I was so embarrassed, but I wasn't even guilty."

Another student said, "It's not good when the teacher is walking around monitoring, and they don't know what you're looking at, so you want to get rid of it as soon as you can." Another agreed, "When it happens, you don't want to look bad in school."

Both librarians interviewed were experienced in dealing with students and controversial sites. Lakeside's librarian said, "It's so widespread, we walk up to them and say 'what did you type in?' We tell them if they come upon an inappropriate site, they should come and tell us because I don't want to see it if I come by there. They say it's a mistake." The librarian in the district's other high school said, "I've never seen a kid pull up pornography, other than someone saying, 'something just happened, help!' I am always walking around with them."

As discussed above, students in both classes stated strongly that they could certainly handle the sites that were being blocked by the filters. They said, "It's not like we're not mature enough not to close it out if something comes up." A Rhetoric student said:

> Even though there is a point that they have the filters in high school because 99% of the kids in school are too immature to handle that kind of thing. But for kids like us, when we're trying to do research, it's not fair to us to go to all the trouble to go home or to another library to look things up just because the kids are too immature to deal with it. We can handle this stuff.

This student would have thought that the Basic Composition students were the ones who were too immature to handle controversial Web sites. But when encouraged to speak for themselves, Basic Composition students claimed it was not them who needed the filter, but other, "immature" students. "It's a pain, but it's necessary because of other immature people, but they could take it down a notch to allow the regular stuff to be unblocked." Again, I wonder where those immature students are. There were none evident in my study.

CHAPTER FIVE

IMPLICATIONS AND SUGGESTIONS FOR FURTHER RESEARCH

The purpose of this study was to describe the experiences of students who conduct term paper research with filtered Internet access in a suburban high school media center. A review of the literature makes it clear that the issue of using filters in school libraries is a critical and controversial dilemma in today's digital environment. Court cases fill the legal literature with decisions at all levels of the legal system on the constitutionality of filters in publicly funded libraries (*Kathleen R v. City of Livermore*, 1999; *Mainstream Loudon v. Board of Trustees*, 1998; *U.S. v. American Library Association*, 2003). Opinion pieces on the merits or demerits of filters abound (Auld, 2003; Gardner, 2002b; Kranich, 2004). A number of studies demonstrate the effectiveness or ineffectiveness of filters used in libraries (Electronic Frontier Foundation and Online Policy Group, 2003; Richardson, 2002; Thornburgh, 2002). What has not been found in the literature is a description of the actual experiences of students who use the Internet for term paper research in high school media centers with filtered computers. This study helps to fill the information gap.

SUMMARY OF FINDINGS

The findings in this study indicate that filters used in high school media centers block legitimate, constitutionally-protected speech. Students experienced frequent "overblocking," that is, the filter blocked sites that were appropriate for school use. Although the school district had established a policy for users to request that a site be unblocked, it was little known, not timely, and therefore, rarely effective. Students in the study were very adept at getting around the filter, utilizing a number of approaches including using an alternate search engine, clicking the "refresh" button, using page translators, changing terminology, and going home to use a personal computer without a filter. Less frequently, students in the study also experienced "underblocking" by the filter, whereby the filter failed to block Web sites with inappropriate content. Students expressed a variety of emotions to describe the way they felt when blocked by the filter. Most often they said they were frustrated, as well as annoyed and angry. A majority of students felt that the school's filter hindered their work in doing Internet research for their papers. A smaller group of students felt that the filter had a negative effect, even though it might be necessary. Very few students of those participating in the study felt the filter had a positive effect. The students had many practical ideas on alternate solutions to filtering, although they had never been asked. Their ideas included different filtering profiles for different classes, or even individual students, giving the teacher authority to turn off the filter, having one unfiltered computer available under teacher supervision, customizing the filter according to age level, and even a trial period without the filter to see what harm could come from it. Students did not feel they were permanently harmed when they came upon an occasional inappropriate Web site. They treated it fairly casually and moved on with their work, although they felt there were other less mature students who perhaps might be more affected.

It was clear that there was a significant disconnect between what the district technology administrator thought was happening in the schools and what actually took place in the media center that I observed. The technology administrator thought that the filter was causing no problems. He said, "If in two years, we've only dealt with nineteen sites, it's not irritating a whole lot of people" and laughed, "… it's not likely to change." However, the study showed that the filter was irritating students, teachers and librarians alike. They were frustrated, annoyed, angered, and felt their time had been wasted. They did not ask to have the filter disabled either because they were not aware of that possibility, or they did not think it would happen in time for their project, if at all.

Directly resulting from the technology's administrator's arrogance, there was an undercurrent of frustration and hopelessness at effecting change by those using the technology. Students had the distinct impression that they were not to be trusted with sensitive information, even though one student told me that what they saw and heard every day in the halls was worse than what was blocked on the screen. Students, teachers, and librarians took the approach that even if they did make a request to have the filter adjusted, it would never happen, or it would take so long that it would become moot. This is not a healthy or productive attitude to engender in students who are about to become the decision-makers in society. If they are taught to give up before they have ever tried to bring about change, democracy has a dismal future.

IMPLICATIONS FOR POLICY AND PRACTICE

School boards across the country must decide whether or not to install and maintain filtering devices on their computers. Strong financial incentives for federal e-rate funding drive many of these decisions. The latest survey done by the National School Boards Foundation (2002) shows that over 90% of school districts filter in some way. The findings in this study suggest that such a decision should be undertaken with care and planning in weighing the benefits and drawbacks. Consideration should be given to the question of whether a filter is necessary—or necessary at all grade levels. District administrators should consider mandatory instructional sessions on Internet safety before they resort to technology protection measures such as filters.

The findings of this study indicate that upper level high school students are capable of using the Internet wisely. Furthermore, when students do come across inappropriate sites, they show mature judgment in moving on. I neither saw nor heard any evidence of harm to a student from the experience of viewing an inappropriate Web site.

The literature from all levels of the field suggests that programs aimed at educating students in effective use of the Internet may be more effective in keeping them safe than technology devices such as filters. In a news report from a high school in Roanoke, VA (Berry, 2003), the author remarked:

> Rather than blocking content that some people find objectionable, schools and parents should teach children critical-thinking skills to help them evaluate content on the Internet and elsewhere. While filtering can be a short-term solution, the ability to analyze information from media sources such as the Internet will last them a lifetime. (p. 2)

From the field of Education, Callister and Burbules (2003) observe:

> Filtering is anti-educational in its *explicit* manifestation because it prevents students from accessing materials

that they might find important, interesting, and relevant to their learning. Perhaps more important, filtering is anti-educational in its *implicit* messages about what adults think about education; it promotes a notion of education steeped in the importance of obedience and acquiescence, while compromising opportunities for independent student questioning and discovery. It manifests a distrust for students and in many cases an exaggerated sense of their vulnerability. As a result, filtering operates counter to what students need to learn in school—to discern, discriminate, synthesize, and evaluate. How can students learn to be responsible, to make good social and intellectual choices, if those choices are made for them by filtering the information they can and cannot access? It is difficult to teach young people self-control and judgment by denying them access to those things about which they need to exercise judgment. (p. 6-7)

The landmark National Research Council study (Thornburgh, 2002) concluded:

The most important finding of the committee is that developing in children and youth an ethic of responsible choice and skills for appropriate behavior is foundational for all effort to protect them ... In short, a child who responsibly chooses appropriate materials to access and appropriate things to do on the Internet and who knows what to do about inappropriate materials and experiences should he or she come across them is much safer than a child whose parents and teachers rely primarily on technology and public policy to solve the problem for them. (p. 365)

The students at Lakeside High School knew this about themselves. They sensed that the administrators in their school did not trust them to recognize and do the right thing. They did not dismiss lightly societal concern for sexually explicit materials on school premises. They understood that some, presumably younger, children may need guidance in sorting out "bad" materials on the Internet. But they resented a poorly conceived and disastrously implemented artificial device that prevented them from accessing needed information without any input into the decision or any effective way to redress inequity.

Lakeside High School may stand as an example of how not to filter. There was obvious lack of communication between the district level administration that mandated and implemented the filter and the students, teachers, and librarians who had to live with the consequences. There was no discussion on the level of filtering that was necessary. Once installed, there was no feedback sought on whether filtering was desirable or effective. There was ample evidence that the filter was seriously and unnecessarily overblocking legitimate material, but there was no reliable, efficient way for this information to get back to district administrators for modification.

The students at Lakeside High School were not irreparably harmed by the presence of restrictive filters because they had other resources at their disposal. Their socioeconomic class allowed them to use computers at home when the computers at school failed them. Not all students in America have that luxury. While the digital divide was not an issue for Lakeside students, it is a very real issue for thousands of students across America whose parents are not white, not rich, and not well-educated.

Libraries in publicly funded institutions can help bridge the digital divide, but not if they are mandated by law to use filters that restrict the flow of constitutionally protected information. If filters stopped at blocking true obscenity, child pornography, and materials legally harmful to minors, few in society would object. But they do not. This study demonstrates that unless careful attention is paid to filter settings and they are monitored closely for overblocking, even innocuous, harmless, and government-sponsored information can be blocked. Even worse, Willard (2003) suggests that the filtering industry is prone to viewpoint discrimination, as well:

> There are many other studies and reports validating concerns that companies are blocking access to sites in a manner resulting in viewpoint discrimination. This viewpoint discrimination may be evident on the face of the category descriptions. For example, sites containing information on homosexuality are blocked in the same category as sexual technique and swinging, or sites addressing nontraditional religions are blocked in the same category as cults and Satanism. (p. 6)

Libraries are meant to achieve many of the same public goods as schooling. Gutmann (1987) describes libraries as, "supplying a good that politics can buy but the market cannot—in the case of libraries, a public culture of learning accessible to all children" (p. 238). Kranich (2001), in her study of libraries as the cornerstone of democracy, asserts:

> Libraries are the only American institutions that make knowledge, ideas, and information freely available to all citizens. They are where people can find differing opinions on controversial questions and dissent from current orthodoxy. They serve as the source for the pursuit of independent thought, critical attitudes, and in-depth information. (p. 83)

This is as true for libraries in public schools as it is for public libraries serving their local communities. But it can only remain true if constitutionally protected information is not filtered out from the public's view. The Internet holds much promise as a way to level the playing field for the disadvantaged (Mack, 2001). A poor child at a computer terminal in a school media center should have the same world of ideas open to her as the rich private school student across the country. In the current environment, I agree with Kranich (2004) who worries that "forcing libraries to choose between funding, equitable access, and censorship means millions of library users will lose, particularly those Americans who reside in the most poverty-stricken areas of the country" (p. 17).

Because librarians are socialized to consider the links between filtering and censorship and the necessary relationship between freedom of access and freedom of expression, they should at least share in the leadership role over technology in schools. Too often, technology administrators (as well as government officials) take the "because we can" approach to security without considering its effects on civil liberties. A shared decision-making process would lead to a more balanced consideration of the right to information and the need for protection.

Guidelines for Decision Making

School districts concerned about preserving access to information in a filtered environment have no shortage of sources to consult. The Consortium for School Networking was formed to promote the use of telecommunications to improve K–12 learning. Their stance is that the decision on whether or not to manage and monitor Internet content should be made at the local level. Their "Safeguarding the Wired Schoolhouse" project is designed to educate school leaders on the issues involved. Their Web site offers a "Checklist for Content Management Decisions" designed to keep school districts from making the same kinds of filtering mistakes that Lakeside did.

On the library side, the American Library Association (ALA) produces similar advice on its CIPA Web site, including "Advice and Resources," "News and Articles," and "Legal History." Having lost its battle to have

CIPA declared unconstitutional on its face, ALA has turned to giving practical advice to libraries that face filtering decisions.

When considering the filtering decision, the following guidelines may be helpful to school district officials:

- Implement educational programming for students, parents, and teachers emphasizing safe and responsible use of the Internet.
- Consider whether a filter is necessary—or necessary at all grade levels. Teacher and librarian supervision may be sufficient.
- Make Internet instruction by librarians a prerequisite for Internet access in schools.
- Gather input from students, teachers, and librarians, as well as parents before implementing filters.
- If the decision is made to filter, begin with settings at the lowest levels possible.
- Institute a procedure that is timely and effective to turn off the filter if it is hindering the teaching and learning process. Empower teachers and librarians with the ability to turn the filter off.
- Check back frequently with students, teachers, and librarians to make sure that the filter is not blocking legitimate and appropriate information. If so, adjust the filter settings.

PROSPECTS FOR GENERALIZABILITY

As with all fine-grained studies, this study will have more applicability to schools that are most similar to Lakeside High in terms of socioeconomic factors. Some may wonder whether broader use of these findings is legitimate for schools where funding for technology and linking to the Internet is an issue, including both rural and urban schools. Technology has not always lived up to its promise of being the "great leveler" but has become another way in which the haves spread the gap with the have-nots, despite massive amounts of spending by the federal government to prevent it. But when filters are deployed in the ham-handed way that this school district has done, in and of themselves they further undermine efforts to close these gaps, especially when all students do not have home access to the Internet and it is required for coursework. Thus it seems likely that when schools have computers available in a media center that teachers use for required coursework, with a filter that makes teens confront the same issues encountered by the students in the Lakeside study, especially if they come from homes where technology access is limited or unavailable, then limits on intellectual freedom will increase.

SUGGESTIONS FOR FURTHER RESEARCH

This study was limited to one high school. Because it was located in a fairly affluent suburb of a major Midwestern city, it came as no surprise that all the students participating in the study had access to computers at home. This meant that there was no evidence of a digital divide, the difference in access to digital information that separates the information-rich from the information-poor. However, it was interesting to note that the students themselves recognized how profound an effect there could be in an environment where students only had access to filtered computers at school. Students at Lakeside High School recognized they could always go home to take advantage of less restrictive access. If students do not have this option and only see what the filter lets through, with no way to expand this access in the case of overblocking or blocking from a political viewpoint, they are left with an incomplete view of the world, the one that the government, in the form of the school, wants them to see. Further research is needed in environments where the digital divide is a daily reality, notably in school districts with a majority of low-income or non-English-speaking students.

Because the filtering system at Lakeside High School was so poorly administered, the effect on students was strongly negative. Overblocking was rampant and student reactions were decidedly hostile. Further research is needed in schools where the filters are set at lower levels, with effective disabling mechanisms, to see if the same frustrations are evident. If any schools can be found that forego e-rate funds and do not filter at all, researchers should determine the amount of sexually explicit material that is found and its impact on students.

CONCLUSIONS

The results of this study suggest that a poorly administered filtering program can seriously hinder student Internet research in a high school setting and cause significant frustration in students. In districts that decide filtering is necessary, communication among students, teachers, librarians, and technology administrators is critically important to minimize the negative effects of Internet filters. Feedback needs to be continually sought from users of the technology. Overblocking needs to be kept to a bare minimum, with a disabling mechanism that is readily available, timely and effective. Because the constitutional rights of students are at stake, districts need to exercise extreme caution that there is no content filtering based on viewpoint. In districts where a digital divide exists, school leaders need to recognize the role of the library in ensuring equal access to information.

At the end of my interview with the technology administrator, he was reflecting that if his assistant administrator had his way, all the filters would be turned off. He concluded by saying, "Personally, I don't care. I'm not the one being blocked. In all these years, I've maybe been blocked three times, and that was all from browsing. At that point, it's more a freedom and ethical issue."

Right. That's the point his students were hoping he would see.

APPENDIX A

RECRUITMENT SCRIPT

"Good morning. My name is *Researcher*. I am a doctoral student at State University. I am conducting a research study at this high school and I am here to ask if any of you are interested in participating in the study. I hope to recruit up to fifteen students from two different classes for the study. If more than fifteen students want to participate, I will draw names out of a hat to select participants.

The purpose of the study is to examine and explore the experiences of high school students as they conduct term paper research using filtered Internet access in the media center.

If you take part in this study, you will be observed up to three times, for one hour each, as you use the computers in the media center to search for information on the Internet for your term paper. You will also be asked to participate in an hour-long group interview with other students in your class. You will be asked questions about how you use the Internet to find information for your term paper. The interview will be tape-recorded and one of the observations may be videotaped. You will be asked to keep an online journal recording your experiences as you use the computer to search for information on the Internet. Logs of your computer usage may be examined by the researcher. Your final term paper will be read by the researcher as part of the documentation for the study. This study will take place during second semester (January – May, 2004).

The possible benefits to you for taking part in this study may include learning more about Internet searching for research purposes and a better understanding of the effects of using filtered Internet access for your schoolwork. Finally, information from this study may benefit other students in the future.

There are no known risks at this time to participants in this study.

For taking part in this study, you will be compensated for your time and inconvenience by a pizza luncheon during the group interview and by a $10 gift certificate to a local restaurant or movie theater for keeping the online journal.

All information collected about you during the course of this study will be kept confidential to the extent permitted by law. You will be identified in the research records by a code number. Information that identifies you personally will not be released without your written permission.

Taking part in this study is voluntary. You may choose not to take part in this study, or if you decide to take part, you can change your mind later and withdraw from the study. You are free to not answer any questions or withdraw at any time.

If you are interested in participating in this study, put your parent or guardian's name and address on the envelope that I am distributing right now. They will be sent an information sheet describing the study in the mail and if they choose, they can send back a form saying they prefer that you do not participate in the study.

Thank you for considering this research project."

Appendix B

Guidelines for Student e-mail Assignment of Internet Search Experiences

- Send at least two e-mails to qualify for the $10 movie gift certificate!

- After you have used the library computers to look for information for your research paper on Friday and Monday, send an e-mail to researcher@stateuniversity.edu briefly describing your experience. Send the e-mail within 24 hours of each search session.

- If you use another computer (at home, another library, etc) to look for information for your research paper, you may also send me and e-mail about that search session.

- If you were blocked by the computer's filter, tell me what term you used and what Web site you were blocked from reaching. Tell me if you were able to use alternate terms to get to that website or if you got to another Web site with the same kind of information.

- If you accidentally reached an "inappropriate" Web site, tell me what term you used and what website you reached. Tell me briefly what made the site "inappropriate." **Remember that your identity is absolutely confidential in this study.**

- You should spend an average of 5-10 minutes on each e-mail.

- If you ever have any questions about what you are supposed to do or about any part of the study, contact me:

Researcher
researcher@stateuniversity.edu
555-555-5555 (work)
555-555-5555 (home)

Thank you for your help!

Appendix C

Protocol for Focus Group Interviews with Students

1. Tell me about the times that the filter would block you during an Internet searching session in the library.

2. Did you find a way to get around the filter to keep it from blocking you?

3. Did you think the filter did more overblocking (blocking innocent sites by mistake) or underblocking (failing to block sites it should block)?

4. Did you ever consider asking to have the administration remove the block so you could get to the site you needed to visit? If not, why not?

5. Have you ever come across a "controversial" Web site by accident? If so, how did you feel about that?

6. Overall, do you think the school filtering policy helps you in your work or hinders you? Explain.

7. What could the school do to improve your experience in finding information for your paper on the Internet?

8. Is there anything else you can think of that might give me information for this study?

Appendix D

Interview Protocol for Teachers

1. How long have you been a teacher?

    How long at this school?

2. Tell me about this research paper assignment.

    How will students use the computers in the media center to search for information for their papers?

3. In your experience with students working on computers in the Library for term paper research, have you observed students encountering any barriers of any kind?

    Like not finding information?

    Finding "inappropriate" sites?

    Being blocked by the filter?

4. What strategies do you see students using to overcome these barriers?

5. What effect, if any, do school filtering policies have on student research?

6. Is there anything else you would like to add for the benefit of this project?

Appendix E

Interview Protocol for Librarians/Media Specialists

1. How long have you been a librarian/media specialist?

   How long at this school?

2. Tell me from your perspective about the research paper assignment for this class.

   How do students use the computers in the media center to search for information for their papers?

3. In your experience with students working on computers in the Library for term paper research, have you observed students encountering any barriers of any kind?

   Like not finding information?

   Finding "inappropriate" sites?

   Being blocked by the filter?

4. What strategies do you see students using to overcome these barriers?

5. What effect, if any, do school filtering policies have on student research?

6. Is there anything else you would like to add for the benefit of this project?

APPENDIX F

1. How long have you been Director of Technology with the district?

2. Tell me about the history of filtering in this district. When did it start? What drove the decision? Whose decision was it? How did it evolve over time?

3. What is the current filtering configuration on the high school media center computers?

4. What input have you had from teachers or staff on the filters and how they work?

5. Are you satisfied with the performance of the filters? Is overblocking or underblocking a concern? Do you have any composite statistics that you could share?

6. What is the future of filtering in this district?

APPENDIX G

DATA SOURCES

Research Questions \\ Data Sources	Participant Observation	E-journal Documents	Teacher Interviews (3)	Librarian Interview (1)	Student Group Interview (15 students, 3 groups)	Logs
Internet Use						
Actors	x	x	x	x	x	x
Place	x	x	x	x	x	x
Activities	x	x	x	x	x	x
Digital Divide		x	x	x	x	
Filters						
Barriers	x	x	x	x	x	x
Strategies to overcome	x	x	x	x	x	x
Outside influence	x	x	x	x	x	
Intellectual Freedom						
Infringement	x	x	x	x	x	x
Harm		x	x	x	x	

APPENDIX H

PROFILE OF BESS FILTER

Company overview

Secure Computing® has been securing the connections between people and information for over 20 years. Specializing in delivering solutions that secure these connections, Secure Computing helps customers create a trusted environment both inside and outside their organizations. We are headquartered in San Jose, California, and have sales offices worldwide.

Mission

To be the premier provider of network security products through superior technology, dedicated customer focus, strong partner relationships, and exceptional services and support.

U.S. Headquarters

San Jose, California

Financial status

Secure Computing is publicly traded on the Nasdaq national Market System under the symbol SCUR. Annual revenues (reclassified for discontinued operations of the Advanced Technology contract revenues):

- 2003 Fiscal Revenues: $76.21M
- 2002 Fiscal Revenues: $61.960M
- 2001 Fiscal Revenues: $48.353M
- 2000 Fiscal Revenues: $34.649M
- 1999 Fiscal Revenues: $22.546M

Market opportunity

Organizations today are expanding their businesses through the Internet daily. In this promising business environment, threats are also increasing right along with growth opportunities. Industry analyst IDC now expects the worldwide revenue for security software to be $14.4 billion by 2007.

Our customers need a secure infrastructure they can rely on. Accordingly, our commitment is to mitigate their risk exposure and protect their information assets from a multitude of threats, including identity theft, intruders, legal liability, security compromises, hackers, malicious software, and viruses.

Solutions

Secure Computing® provides a broad range of products to protect and manage assets across the enterprise.

SmartFilter

Secure Computing's SmartFilter products enable organizations to understand and monitor their Internet use, while taking effective steps to provide appropriate control over outbound Web access. The SmartFilter filtering line includes:

- SmartFilter® : offers leading filtering speeds, numerous On-Box configurations, and cost savings with no additional hardware requirements.
- Bess® : is the #1 Web filtering application for education in over 40% of US schools and libraries, offering custom education categories.
- Sentian™ : features delegated administration and multiple off-box deployment options for flexible enterprise content management.

Patents

Secure Computing is a leader in advanced research and development of network and systems security technology. Our team of distinguished scientists and researchers has achieved numerous breakthroughs in the security industry over the past 16 years. The company has been granted a total of 25 patents and currently has 30 patents pending. These patents cover systems architecture, cryptography, electronic mail filtering, and security control systems.

Customers

Secure Computing's customers operate some of the largest and most sensitive networks and applications in the world. They include the majority of the Dow Jones Global 50 Titans and numerous organizations in the Fortune 1000, as well as banking, financial services, healthcare, telecommunications, manufacturing, public utilities, schools, and federal and local governments. Secure Computing has close relationships with the largest agencies of the United States government, including multiple contracts for advanced security research. Overseas, our customers are concentrated primarily in Europe, Japan, China, the Pacific Rim, and Latin America.

Partners

Our partnerships include a global network of OEMs, members of our Secure Alliance program, resellers, systems integrators, and companies that include our solutions in their product offerings. We offer our partners extensive support through our PartnersFirst Program and Web site. All business except for a select group of key accounts are sold through our partners. These companies include Alternative Technologies, Blue Coat Systems, Cisco, Computer Associates, Crossbeam, CSC, Dell, EDS, F5 Networks, Finjan, Hewlett- Packard, Network Appliance, NetOne Systems, Northrop Grumman, Radware, SafeNet, Sun PS, Tech Data, Vertex Link, Volera, Wavecrest Computing, Westcon, and 3Com.

http://securecomputing.com/index.cfm?skey=233&pf=1

REFERENCES

American Association of School Librarians & Association for Educational Communications and Technology. (1988). *Information power: Guidelines for school media programs.* Chicago: American Library Association.

American Association of School Librarians & Association for Educational Communications and Technology. (1998). *Information power: Building partnerships for learning.* Chicago: American Library Association.

Ashcroft v. American Civil Liberties Union, 124 S. Ct. 2783 (2004).

Auld, H. (2003). Filters work: Get over it. *American Libraries, 34*(2), 38-42.

Ayre, L.B. (2004, March/April). Filtering and filter software. *Library Technology Reports, 40*(2), 1-80.

Berry, E. (2004, April 7). Education, not filtering, is the solution. *Roanoke Times.* Retrieved April 8, 2004, from http://www.roanoke.com/roatimes/news/story165248.html

Board of Education, Island Trees Union Free School District No. 26 v. Pico, 457 U.S. 853 (1982).

Callister, T.A., & Burbules, N.C. (2003). *Just give it to me straight: A case against filtering the Internet.* Retrieved September 5, 2003, from http://faculty.ed.uiuc.edu/burbules/ncb/papers/straight.html

Cattagni, A., & Farris, E. (2001, May). *Internet access in U.S. public schools and classrooms: 1994-2000* (NCES 2001-071). Retrieved from U.S. Department of Education. Office of Educational Research and Improvement. National Center for Education Statistics: http://nces.ed.gov/pubsearch/pubsinfo.asp?pubid=2001071

Charmaz, K. (2000). Grounded theory: Objectivist and constructivist methods. In N.K. Denzin and Y.S. Lincoln (Eds.), *Handbook of qualitative research* (2nd ed., pp. 509-535). Thousand Oaks, CA: Sage.

Comer, A.D. (2005, June). Studying Indiana public libraries' usage of Internet filters. *Computers in Libraries, 25*(6), 10-15.

Consortium for School Networking. (2003). *Safeguarding the wired schoolhouse.* Retrieved November 10, 2003 from http://safewiredschools.cosn.org

COPA Commission. (2000, October 20). *Final report of the COPA Commission presented to Congress, October 20, 2000.* Retrieved November 1, 2001, from http://www.copacommission.org/report

Craver, K. (1998). Internet search skills for the college-bound. *School Library Journal, 44*(11), 32-35.

Creswell, J.W. (2002). *Educational research: Planning, conducting, and evaluating quantitative and qualitative research.* Upper Saddle River, NJ: Merrill Prentice Hall.

Curry, A., & Haycock, K. (2001). Filtered or unfiltered? *School Library Journal, 47*(1), 42-7.

DeBell, M., & Chapman, C. (2003, October). *Computer and Internet use by children and adolescents in 2001: Statistical analysis report* (NCES 2004-014). Retrieved from U.S. Department of Education. Institute of Education Sciences. National Center for Education Statistics: http://www.nces.ed.gov/pubs2004/2004014.pdf

Denzin, N.K., & Lincoln, Y.S. (Eds.). (2000). *Handbook of qualitative research.* (2nd ed.). Thousand Oaks, CA: Sage.

Electronic Frontier Foundation & Online Policy Group. (2003, June). *Internet blocking in public schools: A study on Internet access in educational institutions.* Retrieved March 10, 2004 from: http://www.eff.org/Censorship/Censorware/net_block_report/

Farmer, L. (2002). Issues in electronic resource services in K-12 school library settings. *Education Libraries, 25*(2), 6-12.

Feds restart filter debate. (2006, March). *School Library Journal, 52*(3), 36.

Flowers, B.F. (1998). *Analyses of acceptable use policies regarding the Internet in selected K-12 schools in the United States. Dissertation Abstracts International, 59*(04), 1021A. (UMI No. 9829095)

Gardner, C. (2001a). *Conflict resolution behaviors among stakeholders in developing and implementing Internet use policies in Pennsylvania public high schools. Dissertation Abstracts International, 62*(05), 1808A. (UMI 3013270)

Gardner, C. (2001b). School libraries and filtering. *Library Administration & Management, 15*(1), 23-5.

Glaser, B., & Strauss, A. (1967). *The discovery of grounded theory* . Chicago: Aldine.

Grant, S. (2002). Using the Web for research. *Teacher Librarian, 29*(5), 17-20.

Gutmann, A. (1987). *Democratic education.* Princeton, NJ: Princeton University Press.

Heins, M. (2001). *Not in front of the children: "Indecency," censorship and the innocence of youth.* NY: Hill and Wang.

Heins, M., & Cho, C. (2001). *Internet filters: A public policy report.* New York: Brennan Center for Justice.

Heins, M., Cho, C., & Feldman, A. (2006). *Internet filters: A public policy report* (2nd ed.). New York: Brennan Center for Justice.

Holton, B., Bae, Y., Baldridge, S., Brown, M., & Heffron, D. (2004, March). *The status of public and private school library media centers in the United States: 1999-2000* (NCES 2004-313). Retrieved from U.S. Department of Education. Institute of Education Sciences. National Center for Education Statistics: http://nces.ed.gov/pubsearch/pubsinfo.asp?pubid=2004313

Hopkins, D. (1998). The school library media specialist and intellectual freedom during the twentieth century. In K.H. Latrobe, (Ed.), *The emerging school library media center: Historical issues and perspectives* (pp. 39-55). Englewood, Colorado: Libraries Unlimited.

Jaeger, P.T., Bertot, J.C., & McClure, C.R. (2004, November). The effects of the Children's Internet Protection Act (CIPA) in public libraries and its implications for research: A statistical, policy, and legal analysis. *Journal of the American Society for Information Science and Technology, 55*, 1131-9.

Johnson, D. (2004, December). Lessons school librarians teach others. *American Libraries, 35*(11), 46-8.

Jones, B.M. (1999). *Libraries, access and intellectual freedom: Developing policies for public and academic libraries.* Chicago: American Library Association.

Jost, K. (2001). Libraries and the Internet: Are filters needed to block pornography? *CQ Researcher, 11*(21), 465-488.

Kaiser, W.A. (2000, Fall). The use of Internet filters in public schools: Double click on the Constitution. *Columbia Journal of Law and Social Problems, 34*(1), 49-77.

Kathleen R. v. City of Livermore, 87 Cal. App. 4th 684 (Cal. App. 1st Dist. 2001).

Kranich, N. (2001). Libraries, the Internet, and democracy. In N. Kranich (Ed.), *Libraries & democracy: The cornerstones of liberty* (pp. 83-95). Chicago: American Library Association.

Kranich, N. (2004, Winter). Why filters won't protect children or adults. *Library Administration & Management, 18*(1), 14-18.

Lance, K.C. (1994). The impact of school library media centers on academic achievement. *School Library Media Quarterly, 22*(3), 167-70.

Lenhart, A., et al. (2003, April 16). *The ever-shifting Internet population: A new look at Internet access and the digital divide.* Pew Internet & American Life Project. Retrieved from http:// www.pewinternet.org/reports/pdfs/PIP_Shifting_Net_Pop_Report.pdf

Levin, D., & Arafeh, S. (2002, August 14). *The digital disconnect: The widening gap between Internet-savvy students and their schools.* Pew Internet & American Life Project. Retrieved from http://www.pewinternet.org/reports/pdfs/PIP_Schools_Internet_Report.pdf

Lincoln, Y. & Guba, E. (1985). *Naturalistic inquiry.* Newbury Park, CA: Sage Publications.

Lorenzen, M. (2001). The land of confusion? High school students and their use of the World Wide Web for research. *Research Strategies, 18*, 151-163.

Mack, R.L. (2001). *The digital divide: Standing at the intersection of race & technology.* Durham, NC: Carolina Academic Press.

Mainstream Loudon v. Board of Trustees of Loudon County Library, 2 F. Supp. 2d 552 (E.D. Va. 1998).

McCombs, G.M. (1998, Spring). The keys of the kingdom have been distributed: An organizational analysis of an academic computing center. *Library Trends, 46*(1), 681-698.

Miller v. California, 413 U.S. 15 (1973).

Minow, M. (2004, April). Lawfully surfing the net: Disabling public library Internet filters to avoid more lawsuits in the United States. *First Monday (Online), 9*(4). Retrieved January 29, 2006, from http://www.firstmonday.org/issues/issue9_4/minow/index.html

Mitchell, K.J., Finkelhor, D., & Wolak, J. (2003, March). The exposure of youth to unwanted sexual material on the Internet: A national study of risk, impact, and prevention. *Youth & Society, 34*(3), 330-58.

Nastasi, B.K. (1999). Audiovisual methods in ethnography. In J.J. Schensul, & M.D. LeCompte (Series Eds.) & J.J. Schensul, M.D. LeCompte, B. K. Nastasi, & S.P. Borgatti (Vol Eds.), *Ethnographer's toolkit:* Vol. 3. *Enhanced ethnographic methods: Audiovisual techniques, focused group interviews, and elicitation techniques* (pp. 1-50). Walnut Creek, CA: Altamira Press.

National Commission on Excellence in Education. (1983). *A nation at risk: The imperative for educational reform: A report to the nation and the Secretary of Education* (GPO 83016997). Washington, DC: U.S. Government Printing Office.

National School Boards Foundation. (2002, June 5). *Are we there yet?* Retrieved November 9, 2002, from: http://www.nsbf.org/thereyet/fulltext.htm

National Telecommunications and Information Administration. (1995). *Falling through the Net: A survey of the "have nots" in rural and urban America.* Washington, D.C. Retrieved August 22, 2003, from http://www.ntia.doc.gov/ntiahome/fallingthru.html

National Telecommunications and Information Administration. (1998). *Falling through the Net II: New data on the digital divide.* Washington, D.C. Retrieved August 22, 2003, from http://www.ntia.doc.gov/ntiahome/net2/falling.html

National Telecommunications and Information Administration. (1999). *Falling through the Net: Defining the digital divide.* Washington, D.C. Retrieved August 22, 2003, from http://www.ntia.doc.gov/ntiahome/fttn99/FTTN.pdf

National Telecommunications and Information Administration. (2000). *Falling through the Net: Toward digital inclusion.* Washington, D.C. Retrieved August 22, 2003, from http://search.ntia.doc.gov/pdf/fttn00.pdf

National Telecommunications and Information Administration. (2003). *Report to Congress: Children's' Internet Protection Act.* Washington, D.C. Retrieved

September 15, 2003, from http://www.ntia.doc.gov/ntiahome/ntiageneral/cipa2003/CIPAreport_08142003.htm

Office for Intellectual Freedom of the American Library Association. (2002). *Intellectual freedom manual* (6th ed.). Chicago: American Library Association.

Peck, R.S. (2000). *Libraries, the First Amendment and cyberspace: What you need to know.* Chicago: American Library Association.

Phoenix council demands filters on all library computers. (2004, October). *American Libraries, 35*(9), 14-16.

Pownell, D., & Bailey, G.D. (1999). Electronic fences or free-range students? Should schools use Internet filtering software? *Learning and Leading with Technology, 27*(1), 50-57.

Reno v. American Civil Liberties Union, 521 U.S. 844 (1997).

Richardson, C.R., Resnick, P.J., Hansen, D.L., Derry, H.A., & Rideout, V.J. (2002). Does pornography-blocking software block access to health information on the Internet? *JAMA, 288,* 2887-2894.

Rodney, M.J., Lance, K.C., & Hamilton-Pennell, C. (2003). *The impact of Michigan school librarians on academic achievement: Kids who have libraries succeed.* Lansing, MI: Library of Michigan. Retrieved from http://www.michigan.gov/documents/hal_lm_schllibstudy03_76626_7.pdf

Rosenberg, R.S. (2001). Controlling access to the Internet: The role of filtering. *Ethics and Information Technology, 3,* 35-54.

Schensul, J.J. (1999). Focused group interviews. In J.J. Schensul, & M.D. LeCompte (Series Eds.) & J.J. Schensul, M.D. LeCompte, B.K. Nastasi, & S.P. Borgatti (Vol Eds.), *Ethnographer's toolkit: Vol. 3. Enhanced ethnographic methods: Audiovisual techniques, focused group interviews, and elicitation techniques* (pp. 51-114). Walnut Creek, CA: Altamira Press.

Schensul, S.L., Schensul, J.J. & LeCompte, M.D. (1999). Semistructured interviewing. In J.J. Schensul, & M.D. LeCompte (Series Eds.) & S.L. Schensul, J.J. Schensul & M.D. LeCompte, (Vol Eds.), *Ethnographer's toolkit: Vol.2: Essential ethnographic methods* (pp. 149-64). Walnut Creek, CA: Altamira Press.

Selverstone, H. (2001). Intellectual and academic freedom vs. filters and challenged materials: Where are you on this continuum? *Knowledge Quest, 29*(3), 5-7.

Shirley, L. (2001). Intellectual freedom in school libraries. *Louisiana Libraries, 64*(2), 17-19.

Splitt, D. (1996, September). Decency vs. free speech: There is no substitute for supervision. *Electronic School.* Retrieved October 30, 2002, from http://www.electronic-school.com/0996f2.html

Spradley, J.P. (1980). *Participant observation.* Fort Worth, TX: Harcourt Brace College Publishers.

Tapscott, D. (1998). *Growing up digital: The rise of the Net generation.* New York: McGraw-Hill.

Thornburgh, D., & Lin, H.S. (Eds.). (2002). *Youth, pornography and the Internet.* Washington, D.C.: National Academy Press.

Trotter, A. (1996, September). Decent exposure: Should schools limit access to the Internet? *Electronic School.* Retrieved October 30, 2002, from http://www.electronic-school.com/0996f1.html

U.S. v. American Library Association, 539 U.S. 194 (2003).

Willard, N. (2002). *The constitutionality and advisability of the use of commercial filtering software in U.S. Public Schools.* Retrieved from http://netizen.uoregon.edu/Constitutionality.pdf

Willard, N. (2003, October). CIPA and the Supreme Court decision: Where are we now? *Multimedia Schools, 10*(5), 6,8.

INDEX